There's Money in This Book: 17 Secrets from a Marketing Mastermind

There's Money in This Book: 17 Secrets from a Marketing Mastermind

By

Karol Clark
Rob Cuesta
Jerry Dreessen
Niki Faldemolaei
JT Ippolito
Steve Laurvick
Sandi Masori

Everett O'Keefe
Cydney O'Sullivan
Dave Pittman
Melodie Rush
Carl Stearns
Steve Walther
Pat Ziemer

Copyright © 2014 by The Marketing Mastermind

Published by The Marketing Mastermind

All rights reserved.

Written permission must be secured from the Authors or Publisher to use or reproduce any part of this book.

ISBN-13: 978-1502382948
ISBN-10: 1502382946

Cover Design: Niki Faldemolaei

Table of Contents

Foreword *by Pat Ziemer* 1

How Strangers Become Buyers—The Client Journey *by Rob Cuesta* 3

The Lifetime Value of a Client *by Everett O'Keefe* 14

Face The Music: You Might Have the Wrong Idea About Marketing *by Carl Stearns* 21

Share Your Expertise: 5 Strategies for Creating an Engaging and Compelling Presentation *by Melodie Rush* 33

Keyword Reasearch *by Jerry Dreessen* 42

How To Create Profit-Pulling Sales Letters FAST... Even If You HATE Writing *by Steve Walther*............. 55

Video Marketing *by Sandi Masori* 77

Mobile Devices and Marketing *by Steve Laurvick* 85

Social Media—Leveraging Your Brand and Creating Buzz *by Jerry Dreessen, Melodie Rush, & Karol Clark* ..102

Trade Shows *by Sandi Masori* 120

Speak To Sell—How To Get People To Buy What You're Selling, Even If They Have No Idea They Want It Or Need It *by Rob Cuesta* 131

7 Ways to Profit from Starring in Your Own Show *by Niki Faldemolaei* 144

Go from Marketing Frustration to Marketing Sensation: 7 Steps to a Successful Crowd Grabber Campaign *by Karol Clark* 155

Reach Your Perfect Audience—Leverage the Power of Facebook Advertising to Target Your Ideal Market *by Dave Pittman* 174

How To Be a Highly Paid Speaker, Trainer, or Coach *by Cydney O'Sullivan* 196

Become an Instant Authority with the Power of Publishing *by Everett O'Keefe*....................................211

Moving Up the Food Chain: Closing Bigger Internet Marketing Clients *by Joe (JT) Ippolito*......................222

Putting it all together: A Case Study—Magna Wave Certification Process *by Pat Ziemer* 231

Final Thoughts 235

Foreword
by Pat Ziemer

I distribute therapy equipment that is used for the relief of pain and inflammation. The primary market we service is that of performance and race horses and we are now moving into the human market, dealing with all forms of pain relief. I asked if I could write the foreword because by utilizing the tools described in this book and the services of many of the contributors, I was actually able to experience a massive growth of my business in just a couple of months when I implemented what I learned from this group and some of their peers. More on my business success will be shared later as a case study. So let me briefly share with you why I think you should carefully read this book and how it can help you grow your business, whether it be as a marketer or as a sole proprietor.

When I started my business seven years ago, its growth was a result of direct sales and contact with my potential customers. The methods worked, but I soon learned that I needed to connect with my customers from all over the country in a timely and efficient manner. So I engaged the Internet and the burgeoning social media outlets, and that is when things got messy. There was so much to learn. And when I would learn what to do, it would change and I found myself starting over again. While the strategy worked and the business continued to grow, after four years the business stagnated in the mid six-figure range. I was drowning in a pool of technical information and strategies from everybody and their brother regarding online marketing strategies.

I found myself buying a product and starting to learn it, but then a week later someone had the next best thing and I would jump in and start over again. My wife called it acting like a squirrel or what many refer to as the shiny object syndrome. In 2011, I purchased a marketing product from Mike Koenigs and once again embarked on the learning and implementation path. The difference this time was that there was a community that I could interact with for questions, support, and actual implementable ideas on how to use the products specifically for the benefit of my company. Along the way, I hired Ed Rush as my business coach and he showed me how to focus and dig deeper into the community mastermind opportunities.

Over the past three years, this association and community has stayed intact and continues to serve as a clearinghouse for online and offline marketing strategies.

If I see something new, I am virtually assured that someone in this group has researched the product and can quickly help me know if it's really for me or not. I have quit chasing shiny objects by using the mastermind functions of this group.

You can do the same by utilizing the information in this book in order to save time and help you maintain your focus on reaching your business goals. So I emphatically encourage you to carefully read this book, reach out to those who fit your needs, and mastermind with others. In doing so, the success you desire will certainly be within your reach. It's been said that it takes five to twelve customer interactions to make a sale or gain a customer. In this book, you will learn how to effectively implement touch strategies from the leaders in the industry that will bring growth to your business. Enjoy, learn, and let me know what you think.

—Pat Ziemer
Magna Wave PEMF

How Strangers Become Buyers—The Client Journey
by Rob Cuestra

A note to readers: this chapter is written by Rob Cuesta, a Brit living in Canada, so you'll need to excuse him if he "incentivises" clients to join his "programmes", etc. It's hard to teach an old dog new tricks, and even harder to teach a Brit to write American ☺

Peter (a real client, but not his real name) was at his wits' end. His boss had recommended he hire me after Peter and his sales team had spent a fruitless summer walking the streets of London (UK), literally door-stepping potential clients in their offices. They were trying to sell a high-end business-to-business service as though it were a vacuum cleaner, and the results were what you would have predicted.

So now we were discussing different ways of finding new clients that would be more effective.

"We have 6,000 leads," he told me.

I was puzzled. With 6,000 leads, why did they spend the summer going door-to-door? So I asked him to show me his database. As soon as he opened the file on his laptop I understood the problem. It was a database he'd bought from a list broker.

"These aren't leads," I said. "These are 6,000 strangers who've never heard of you and for all you know have absolutely no interest in what you're offering. Let me show you what I mean"

As I drew out the model I'll be sharing with you in this chapter, Peter's eyes opened—literally and metaphorically. By the end of our hour together, he had started to create a spreadsheet to track potential clients through their journey from strangers to buyers and beyond, and he was eager to share it with his sales team.

Mastering the ideas I shared with him that day, and over the six months that we worked together, allowed Peter and his team to switch from chasing strangers in the hope they'd spend a few hundred or a couple of thousand dollars to generating six hot, qualified leads that together were worth over $1.7 MILLION.

And central to the whole transformation was understanding what I call the Client Journey. The Client Journey is where sales and marketing meet.

Traditionally, marketing has been seen as being all about building awareness of your product or service, or even just general awareness of your business and brand, while sales has been all about closing the deal. So at some point there had to be a hand-off. The potential buyer had enough awareness and it was time for the sales people to take over and get the sale.

The best way I can think of to explain it is this: think about how you bought groceries back in 2000. You were bombarded with marketing messages from Walmart (or your supermarket of choice) that told you all about their products, their latest offers, their store locations—everything they needed you to know to be ready to buy. But you weren't buying. You weren't buying until you got in your car, drove to Walmart, grabbed a shopping cart, filled it up and took it to the cash register.

Everything that happened until you walked through Walmart's door was marketing. Everything that happened once you were inside was sales.

Now compare that to shopping today. You see a flyer for Walmart and you start up your laptop or tablet. You add something to your cart and the system suggests other items you might be interested in. It may even suggest some more special deals you hadn't noticed. If something isn't in stock it suggests alternatives.

You're being sold to and marketed to at the same time.

In the UK, Sainsbury's supermarket has even managed to bring this to the in-store experience. As you walk in you scan your loyalty card and the system churns out a dozen vouchers based on your shopping history and what they have in-store that day.

You're being sold to and marketed to at the same time. The handover from marketing to sales never really happens.

The ultimate example of the new approach to sales is Ikea.

Think about how different it is from a traditional furniture retailer. The people walking into a typical furniture retailer are there to make a specific purchase. They may be looking for help to choose a specific bed or dining table, or they may even have made a choice already from a flyer and they are there just to check that it's OK in the real world and not just on paper. Either way they are there with a purchase.

The typical Ikea shopper is there to explore. They may even be there just for the legendary meatballs and to see what's new in store. In the UK it's often difficult to get a catalogue in-store at Ikea. I'm convinced that is because they don't want you to do your shopping in your armchair: they want you to walk into the store and discover.

In a typical furniture retailer you can wander around as you please, visit departments in any order, you can even skip everything and go straight to the order desk if you know what you want.

In Ikea there's a route. It starts with the instantly recognisable blue box building with its yellow logo that calls to you from the roadside. It's been carefully planned to take you past as many items as possible. Sure, you can skip the children's department, but that's about it. And the order desks are right at the end of the store, after they've walked you past their entire catalogue and you've had a chance to make every possible purchase. And in case you've still got some cash in your account after shopping, there's the food store AFTER the cash registers.

It is as carefully orchestrated as a Beethoven symphony, and a lot more profitable. Ikea has created an experience that is designed to take someone who can't even spell Ikea and turn them into a raving fan. They have mastered the Client Journey.

You see, the biggest mistake I see businesses making is not understanding how someone who has never heard of the business before is going to go from total lack of knowledge to reaching into their wallet or bank account and buying from you. And beyond that, how do you turn them into a loyal, repeat buyer—even more importantly—how do you get them to refer other potential buyers to you.

In fact, there are four big hurdles your buyer has to cross along the way, and nine distinct stages they go through to get there. At each stage your potential buyer is looking for something different.

Think of the stages as nine decisions the buyer must make. Each decision requires different information, and at each stage you need to treat the potential buyer differently. If you want to kill your business quickly and efficiently (though unfortunately not without a lot of pain), treat everyone the same and don't give them the information they need. And if you don't understand the Client Journey then there's a better-than-90% probability that you're doing exactly that.

Let me give you a very simple example that shows you exactly what I mean.

Imagine you've opened a gift shop by the sea, selling beautiful, high-end gifts from around the world. You're in a prime location, and every day thousands of people walk past your door. They are complete **STRANGERs**. They don't know who you are or what you do, and they have no idea why they would want to walk through your door.

So your first job has to be to *attract* them into the shop. You set up the shop window displays, you hand out flyers, advertise in the local paper—whatever it takes to tell people you're there and get them through the door. You may even set up deal with local hotels to send you visitors.

Of course, if you get that messaging wrong people will still walk past, or the wrong people will be attracted to the store. After all, this is a gift shop by the beach. Some people may have come in expecting to buy cheap plastic sunglasses and a cheesy T-shirt (you know the ones: "my dad went to the beach and all he brought me back was this cheap T-shirt"). That's not the kind of gift shop you're running.

But let's assume for now that you understand your market, you know who you're trying to attract and what will get them to step through your door. If you've got that right then some of those Strangers will walk into the shop and become **VISITORs**.

What's your job now?

You need to *interest* them enough to get them to stay. If they arrive at your shop and they don't see anything to interest them they will turn right around and walk out (as it happens, if that was your website then you typically have 8 seconds. After that, 50% of your visitors will click away and they're unlikely to come back).

Now, at this stage a clueless shop owner might send in a member of staff to try to sell to them. Too early: the person has literally just walked in the door, so there's a good chance you'll scare them away because they aren't committed to even staying in the shop yet, let alone buying from you!

So you need to keep them interested. You set up some bright, eye-catching displays, you put out some samples. Some people still turn around and walk out—this just wasn't the shop for them. But some of them stay. They walk in and pick up one of the samples you set out.

At this point it's fair to **SUSPECT** that they are a good potential customer for your stop. They've crossed the first major hurdle: by picking something up to inspect it, they've signalled that this is potentially interesting to them. It's almost as though they held up their hand to say "yes, I'm interested".

This is a good time to start preparing the potential buyer for the kind of prices you charge. You need to *educate* them about what to expect. So, next to the samples you have panels that explain that the rug in their hand was woven from the belly button fluff of 1,000 Alpacas in the Andes. The fluff is 200 times softer and 30 times more thermally efficient than the goat hair used for most rugs. Also, part of the profits from each sale goes to support workers' co-operatives in Central America. So their purchase will save them money on heating, save wear and tear on their socks, and make them feel better for having helped struggling peasant craftsmen.

You could even get one of your staff to share all this, but beware: this is still not the time to try to sell! If you do, they may well turn and run. This is a phase for education. Let the buyer *sell themselves* the idea of buying from you.

If they browse the shelves, pay attention to the educational pieces you've set up and they're still interested, then they're actually a good **PROSPECT**.

Now it's time to check whether they're actually in the right shop. Who are they shopping for? Is it for themselves? A friend? A loved one? What's important to them when choosing a gift? Did they have anything specific in mind? How much were they planning on spending? And so on.

Your objective is to *qualify* them: are they actually likely to make a purchase today? If they are, then now—and only now— do they become a good **LEAD**.

A list of 6,000 names you bought from someone is not a list of leads, even though many businesses act as though they are. A single person standing in front of you telling you that they need what you're selling, they want to buy and they can afford to buy: that's a lead!

So now you can *engage* them. Keep the conversation going. Find out more about them. Show them how the different gifts in your shop meet their criteria, and will make them loved by whoever is the lucky recipient of the gift they eventually buy.

Eventually they'll settle on something specific. This is your **OPPORTUNITY**. They're telling you this is the kind of thing they're looking for. Now you just need to *persuade* them to become a **BUYER**.

Getting them to make that first purchase is the second big hurdle you need your buyer to cross. And most gift shops would let them walk out now, happy that they'd made a sale.

Another mistake.

The first dollar you get from a buyer is always the hardest. It requires the most work by you, and the most trust by them. After that first purchase, every other sale will be easier. So you owe it to yourself to make those future sales.

There are other people in your customer's life who they may want to buy gifts for. They may even buy something for themselves. It's just that *today* they don't need anything else. But unless you make the effort, you're not going to be able to *resell* them and turn them into a **REPEAT BUYER**.

So you set up a mailing list. You offer to remind them of upcoming birthdays and special events, and send them hand-selected gifts to match the person and the occasion.

Getting someone to come back and make a repeat purchase is the third big hurdle. Getting them to buy once proves you're good at sales, you're good at making promises. Getting them to buy again proves you're great at delivering what you promised. If you weren't they wouldn't have bought again.

So you need to get that repeat sale, just so you know you're doing well!

And even if they do buy again, you're still not done: they know other people who buy gifts. And those people probably have similar tastes to their own (that's why they are friends!). But don't assume that just because of that, they are going to refer those friends to you. Thinking that people are going to refer their friends to you just because you've got great products or services and you provide exceptional customer service is arrogant, lazy, and foolish.

Referring someone is the fourth and final hurdle your buyer must cross. It shows that

1. they find your offer interesting (they "held up their hand")
2. you make promises they see value in (they bought)
3. you deliver on your promises (they bought again)
4. you do that so consistently that they will trust you to do the same for their friends

But if you leave it to them then there's a good chance that either

- they won't think to refer someone, even when the opportunity arises; or
- they will refer someone, but it's the wrong person. That person won't see the value in working with you, they'll say that to your original customer who will feel so bad they won't refer anyone ever again.

So first, you need to make sure that your customers have a good reason to send you their friends. That might be a financial incentive, special deals, rewards—we've helped out own clients set up all sorts of incentive programmes for referrals.

Second, you need to make sure that your customers know who to send to you and when. You need to train them to look out for the right people with the right problem, who are of the right mindset. And we need to tell them what to say. All too often we assume that just because someone is already our customer, they know what we are looking for in a referral. They don't. But if we can help them to understand what makes a good referral for us, and just as importantly how to presell us to that referral, we are onto a winner.

In other words: if you want someone to make referrals you need to *incentivise and train* them to become a **REFERRER**.

And of course they are going to send you people who are strangers, who you need to attract into your business, to educate, qualify and engage, up to the point where you can persuade them to buy, then you'll have to resell them and train and motivate them to refer others.

The cycle repeats and that's how your shop grows, until one day you franchise the business model, and retire to a boat in the Bahamas (or whatever your dream is).

I don't care if you run a seaside gift shop, a law or accounting firm, or a dental practice: your business works exactly the same way I just described. You attract people to your business, you have to interest them, educate them, qualify and engage them. Then you need to persuade them to become a client or customer, you keep reselling them further purchases, and you have to get them to refer you to more potential buyers. At each stage you need to treat them differently, and give them what they need to decide to move to the next stage.

And there's one more mistake business owners make: they assume the people who walk out at any stage aren't interested. The reality is that some of them *aren't* interested. They may have been looking for a cheap t-shirt. But some of them may have realised that they're late to meet a friend at a bar nearby, or their partner may have shouted for them to catch up, or they may have been distracted by something. You don't know.

These are people who you invested in. You paid to attract them. You advertised. You hired a window dresser to set up the displays. You went out and grabbed people off the streets if you needed to. You did whatever it took to get them to your shop (or website, or chambers, or practice or wherever you do business).

Letting them walk out with no way to follow up with them is a waste of that investment.

Here's a scary statistic. 99% of visitors to a typical website will leave without buying a thing. Think about what that means for a moment.

Let's assume you're doing Pay Per Click advertising (and if you're not then we need to talk seriously about why you should!). And let's say you're pleased with yourself because you're only paying $1 a click for every person who sees your ad and follows the link to your site.

If 99 out of every 100 visitors to your site is going to leave empty handed then your cost per click isn't $1. It's $100. That's a **big** difference. It's a difference you need to care about. And it's a difference you need to understand.

That's why you need to understand the Client Journey; you need to track where people are in their journey; and you need to put in place mechanisms that will let you stay in touch with the 99% of visitors who are leaving your site without buying.

> **BONUS**
> To download a copy of Rob's free guide to optimising your online presence so potential buyers move through the Client Journey faster and more profitably, visit
> http://0s4.com/r/TMITB3.

About the Author

Rob Cuesta is an expert in online brand optimisation, sales funnel acceleration and customer value maximisation, based in Toronto, Canada.

Rob is the owner of Joined-Up Marketing and HyperSuasion Consulting, and the author of three Amazon best-selling books on marketing for professionals. With a client base that spans four continents and over 25 years' experience as a speaker, consultant and marketer, Rob has worked with some of the largest organisations in the world and some of the smallest.

"A lot of money gets wasted by businesses every year on marketing that, quite frankly, doesn't work. After completing my MBA at a top European business school I realised that what was missing from a lot of the standard marketing approaches was a way of showing a direct link from marketing to revenue. Business owners were screaming 'show me the money!' and marketers couldn't. Or wouldn't. So I made myself a promise: to only use marketing techniques—for myself and for my clients—that would directly drive money into the business."

As the creator of the Joined-Up Digital Marketing System, Rob's promise is simple: to help you add an extra zero to your income by positioning you as the leading expert in your field and then developing marketing funnels that convert total strangers into buyers, repeat buyers, and ultimately into referrers.

All on autopilot.

WARNING: working with Rob may expose you to revolutionary ideas, untapped revenue streams and extreme profitability. You have been warned!

The Lifetime Value of a Client
by Everett O'Keefe

You are going to learn some wonderful strategies and tactics in this book. I know each of these experts personally, and I have seen them in action. They know their stuff, and they DO what they are talking about. They don't just talk about it, like so many experts are prone to do. So look forward to the rest of this book with anticipation.

But as important as these different techniques can be, they are useless if you don't understand the value of a client to your business. Jumping into a book project (which I write about later), or creating a podcast, or working trade shows without a solid understanding of what a new client is worth is like buying a car without verifying that it runs. You are essentially "buying" new clients with your marketing and sales efforts without knowing whether these clients are actually worth having! At best, you are shooting in the dark if you don't know the lifetime value of a customer.

Now, if you do not know what a new client or customer is worth to your business, let me first help you by sharing this. Not a single prospective business client of mine has ever had a good grasp on this. They may have thought they did when I first asked them about the value of a client, but a few questions later, after a few intelligent questions, a look of enlightenment creeps over their face. So please do not beat yourself up if you don't have a good grasp on this. But DO take steps to fill this blind spot if you have it.

One of my favorite parts of meeting with a new client is to walk them through the Lifetime Value of a Client exercise. This is something I learned from Speaker/Consultant/Fighter Pilot Ed Rush. I have put my own touches on the exercise after using this with several clients, but the general idea and purpose remains the same. In just a few minutes, a business owner and

I can narrow down the true value of a client. Here is how it works:

Think of your own business. Think of the typical new client. Not your favorite or most lucrative one, and not the worst one, but a typical or average new client. Do you have this person in mind? Great. Now answer these questions IN ORDER, and do the math as you go along. If you need to, write the answers on a separate piece of paper so you can make some calculations.

One more thing. Be conservative in your answers. Don't give some pie-in-the-sky valuation when talking about the first- or fifth-year value of a client. Shoot a bit low. For example, if you feel pretty solid about a $500 valuation for something, use $450 or $400 instead. If you think 20% of clients will refer someone at some point, use 15% for your calculations instead. Here is why. When you reach them, the ultimate result may be higher than you expect. So you need to have confidence in this number! If you are overly optimistic, or even right down the middle as you complete this exercise, you will doubt your result. But if you are conservative, you will feel confident that you will earn *at* least the number you come up with. So be a little stingy when it comes to estimating these numbers.

To make this easier, I have created the *Value of a Client Calculator*. Just fill in the blanks and you will have your result! To get it, just send an email to ValueofAClient@TheSolutionMachine.com. My system will instantly send it your way to you can calculate the value of a client "on the fly!"

LIFETIME VALUE OF A CLIENT QUESTIONNAIRE:

1. How much does a new customer spend with you on your initial transaction?

2. What is your profit from that exchange?

3. What percentage of new customers will engage with you in another transaction? If you don't have a solid idea, guesstimate, but be conservative. Err on the low side.

4. Of customers that engage with you beyond the first transaction, how much will they spend with you over the first year? Be conservative.

5. What is your first-year profit from this typical new client?

6. FIRST-YEAR VALUE OF A TYPICAL CUSTOMER: Multiply #3 by #5

7. What percentage of customers engage with you/buy from you for a SECOND year?

8. What will you profit from a typical customer in the second year?

9. SECOND-YEAR VALUE OF A TYPICAL CUSTOMER: Multiply #7 and #8

10. What percentage of customers engage with you/buy from you for a THIRD year?

11. What will you profit from a typical customer in the third year?

12. THIRD-YEAR VALUE OF A TYPICAL CUSTOMER: Multiply #10 and #11

13. What percentage of customers engage with you/buy from you for a FOURTH year?

businesses have very substantial sales and marketing budgets targeting new customers, but have next to no budget for keeping existing ones.

Want to carry out a great test in your organization? Take 10% of what you spend on sales and marketing and place that money in efforts to increase retention. Give some extra love to your customers. Show them they are special and that they are valued by you and your organization, and then watch what happens. You WILL be pleasantly surprised.

And keep this in mind: any improvement in retention increases the average lifetime value of a client. If you increase the percentage of clients that work with you for more years, this can dramatically increase the "subtotal value" of a client. And happy customers also tend to refer others more often. So showing existing clients some extra attention also increases the "referral value" of a client. Even better yet, happy customers tend not only to refer more people, but they tend to refer *better* customers, ones likely to stay with you longer. All told, a little money spent on retention can have an exponential effect on the lifetime value of a client, and, therefore, have a dramatic effect on your bottom line as well.

Calculate the lifetime value of your clients now! Send an email to ValueofAClient@TheSolutionMachine.com to receive Everett's *Value of a Client Calculator*. You can quickly and accurately determine how much your clients are *really* worth to you!

About the Author

Everett O'Keefe is the co-author of the Amazon #1 Bestseller *The Video Tractor Beam: Dominate Your Field and Attract New Clients and Customers with Online Video*. He and his business partner, John Riding, founded The Solution Machine, a cross-channel marketing company focusing on creating new experts and assisting experienced experts with product creation and back-end systems. Everett is certified in a wide variety of marketing strategies and tools, and these tools are "force multipliers" for him and his clients. As of this writing, Everett has helped create and/or launch a total of 8 Amazon bestsellers for his clients, including the 2013 debut of *The Way of Wealth* by Frank Leyes, which reached #1 Bestseller at Amazon in the highly competitive category of Money Management, besting books by Suze Orman, Dave Ramsey, and Clark Howard. His book and CD launches include 5 Amazon #1 bestsellers for his clients. Everett and his team continue to perform video production, product creation, and launches while allowing their clients to focus on their own areas of unique giftedness.

He can be contacted at www.TheSolutionMachine.com or info@TheSolutionMachine.com.

Face The Music: You Might Have the Wrong Idea About Marketing
by Carl Stearns

What should marketing do for your company? Have you considered that question? Have you given it more than a brief moment of thought before you bought into the latest marketing campaign?

The fact is, most business owners don't give it much thought at all. If I asked 25 people what they thought marketing should do for their business, I can just about guarantee you that I would get 25 plus different answers. The responses would most likely include:

- Build brand recognition,
- Position myself and business in the marketplace,
- Generate leads for my salespeople,
- Increase sales conversions,
- Get my products and services more exposure,
- Build top-of-mind awareness of my business, and
- The list would go on.

All of these answers are correct to a point. After all, it's how we've all been "taught" to think of marketing by the countless television, radio, newspaper, and direct mail advertising we experience day in and day out since we were born. Anyone reading this book right now could recite at least a dozen jingles or catch phrases from nationally advertised products and services:

- "I'm Lovin It" – McDonalds.

- "Waking up with Folgers in Your Cup" – Folgers Coffee.

- Just Do It! – Nike.

- "Melts in your mouth, not in your hands" – M&M's.

- "Please don't squeeze the Charmin?" Old Mr. Whipple hasn't run this commercial since 1985, yet we still remember it.

So if this type of marketing and advertising is so effective, why would I suggest you not model it in your advertising?

The reason this brand building/top-of-mind awareness approach to marketing works for these companies is because they have the multimillion dollar budgets necessary to make them work. The campaign depends on repeating the messages a countless number of times for years on end through just about every media choice we have, to the point where we have no choice but to remember them. This repetition requires an incredibly large advertising budget to pull off. McDonald's spent more than $988 million on advertising in 2013.[1] This is why we don't suggest our clients model their marketing strategy after the brand builders. Yes, it works, but it requires way too much upfront capital. Even in a small local market, you are competing with these major corporations' campaigns to get attention.

Building your brand should certainly be a part of your marketing strategy. However, I'd like to suggest you change your mindset right now, or at least consider it, regarding the purpose of marketing in your business beyond branding.

What Does a Trumpet Have to Do With Marketing?

Be a teacher in your marketing.

Yes, that's right—a teacher. Let me explain with this personal story.

My daughter attended a charter school this past year. One of the pleasantly surprising benefits of the school was that it had an incredible music program. My daughter, with very little encouragement or research on her part, decided she wanted to play the trumpet, evidently influenced by the *Little Einsteins* cartoon as a little girl. So every day of the school week, she attended band class for one hour. At first, we could barely stand to hear her practice. Her 5-year-old brother would scream and run from the room any time she took her trumpet out of the case. As good parents, we both said, "That was nice dear," but frankly I wanted to join my son in a mad rush from the house.

After about four weeks, she started getting pretty darn good at this thing. Now we were calling grandpa and grandma so she could play for them and posting videos of her on Facebook. Two months into the school year and we're attending the band recital, and I couldn't believe how good they sound. By the end of the year, this group of brand new music students, along with my daughter, sound like an orchestra.

Now let me get to the marketing point of the story. The school year is done, and my daughter must turn in her rental instrument. She asks me if I would buy her a trumpet to practice with over the summer. "Well, of course honey, no problem." Wide-eyed and dreaming of my musically "gifted" daughter playing Beethoven all summer on her gleaming new trumpet, I am suddenly in the trumpet market.

Looking into buying this trumpet, I discover there are unlimited choices ranging from $100 to $5000. Whoa...I'm certainly not in the market for a $5000 trumpet at this point, but how do I know which trumpet would give my daughter the right platform to further her skills? The fact is, I don't know the first thing about trumpets. I've never purchased a single trumpet in my life to make any type of decision beyond trying to get the lowest price. Go ahead and search "Student Trumpets" on Amazon.com, and you will see what I mean.

I have a problem. I need a trumpet, but have no experience or knowledge on how to buy a trumpet. Amazon.com is no help at all because it's just a list of instruments (Not much different than the way most businesses list their products for sale). About all I can do is sort them from low to high price. The only marketing on the page that is of any help at all is that first one listed is the #1 Best Seller at $119.99. Not to mention the reviews on each of the products are by people, just like me, that probably don't know jack diddly about buying trumpets.

Well, to make a long story at bit shorter, I forwarded the list to my daughter's teacher, who just happened to know a lot about trumpets. Before becoming a "miracle-working" middle school music teacher, he was a professional trumpet player. With his brief instruction, I found a high-quality used trumpet for about $500 that the previous owner used to get a full-ride college scholarship. Daddy can dream.

Ok—so what is the point of the story? What does buying a trumpet have to do with marketing your products and services? Well...everything!

Take a moment to consider what business you're in. What do you sell? What services do you provide? How much do you know about that service or product? Are you an expert when it comes to that product or service? Of course, you are.

How about your prospective customers? How much do they know about your product or service? What do they know about buying that product or service? Are they experts in your field? Do they know as much about your industry as you do? Well...of course not. They are just like me when I got into the trumpet market. They know nothing or worse yet, they might think they know a lot more about it than they do.

That's why it is important for you to become a teacher in your marketing. Sure, a big part of marketing is getting people's attention, but what you do after that is what separates you from the rest of your industry. Teach your prospects about what is critical to their making a good decision when considering buying products or services in your industry. Teach them the difference between a poor deal and a great deal. Give them the knowledge they need to recognize a good value rather than the lowest price.

Customers all want the same thing, no matter what industry you are in. They want the best deal possible. They want to be confident in knowing that they got much more value from their purchase than they paid. It's your job, through your marketing, to help them recognize that your product or service is the best deal and the only way to go, regardless of price. If that is not the case, then change your product or service so that it is and market it that way.

Three steps that should influence how you think about your marketing:

First – Get your prospective customer's attention.

Yes, you can do this with cute kids or sexy models, but I'd rather see you use headlines and imagery that speaks to the problem your product or service solves.

For example, "The #1 Thing Successful Business Owners Do To Attract The Best Salespeople."; "Selling Your Home? Make this Common Mistake, and Your Home is Likely to Sit on the Market for Months Without a Single Offer."; or "Home Improvement Contractors: Put an extra $5,000 of pure profit in your pocket on each and every job for the next 12 months."

Using the problem-focused headlines and imagery will get the attention of prospective customers that are currently experiencing those issues, leading them to the next stage of your marketing.

Next – Promise to TEACH them

Teach them what they need to know to make the best decision possible when considering products and services in your industry. This is critical. This is what gets qualified prospects to engage you. Don't waste the opportunity with common advertising buzzwords like Quality Service, Best Customer Service, Professional Staff, Locally Owned and Operated, Over 2000 Years' Experience, Licensed and Insured, Fast Friendly Service, Honest, Outstanding Results, Hardest Working Staff in the Business, and so on. Frankly any of your competitors can say these phrases in their marketing and therefore these phrases mean absolutely nothing. Worse yet…using them means you're the same as everyone else.

Here is an example of copy that promises to teach. "Did you know that the number one reason homes don't sell in any market throughout the US is the home is not priced right? Naturally, you and your real estate agent want the highest price possible. But price your house wrong, and it will sit on the market for months, or you'll end up giving up a huge portion of your hard-earned equity. You don't have to make this critical home sellers' mistake; learn some straightforward simple things you can do to be confident that your home is priced right in this market…"

Finally – Get them to take a small low-risk action.

You have their attention. You whet their appetite for learning more by promising to teach them industry insider information. Now you need to get them to take action. Most business marketers go for the sale at this point, and in some cases that is perfectly acceptable. In most cases, it's better to just get them to take a small step to show their interest. This is where an easy-to-do, low-risk offer comes into play.

Rather than say "Call me today to schedule a personal appointment. (Not easy – high risk)" try something like "Call (xxx) xxx-xxxx to receive a free copy of my Home Sellers Guide: "5 Things You Should Know Before You Let a Real Estate Agent Price Your Home." Better yet, in addition to calling, give your prospects several ways to request a guide, such as a form on your website, texting in the request, leaving their name and email in a voicemail, email, or scanning a QR code.

Deliver Using Digital Integration

As a digital marketing consultant, I love the benefits of integrating traditional marketing techniques with digital marketing techniques. And this is the perfect opportunity to do exactly that.

Digital integration offers many benefits to just about any type of marketing campaign. The two main advantages are automation and tracking.

1. Automation

When it comes to follow-up on traditional and online marketing campaigns, nothing beats automation for consistency, affordability, and ultimately conversion. A successful marketing campaign, especially when it is set up in the manner described above, requires consistent and persistent follow-up to get sales. And, if human beings are anything, they are certainly not as consistent and persistent as an automated computer program. Here are some ways automated follow-up could be incorporated into your marketing campaigns.

Use online landing pages for all of your marketing campaigns. I don't care if you're sending out a series of postcards or appearing on Fox News. Create landing pages or even a full website to direct people to and capture leads.

Landing pages should include copy that expands on the ideas presented in the campaign's advertising. The landing pages must include at a minimum an opt-in form requesting name and email address, with a phone number as an option. From there, our automated systems can deliver the free report, a buyer's guide, or a sale incentive such as a coupon code directly to their email inbox or text it to their mobile phone. Here is where the magic happens.

Not only do we deliver the promised report or cherished coupon, we now put that person's contact into a system that will consistently and persistently send that contact a series of emails over the next (however many) weeks that make sense for the program. Additionally, we set up the automation program to be "smart" enough to notify you or your sales staff when it might be a good time to call the prospect personally. We would also program the system to recognize a sale and move that person to another series of messaging that makes sense for them continuing into the future.

Here is an example of an automated follow-up campaign we developed for a client.

The client has one product that comes in different lengths. It is a gutter guard product intended to keep leaves and debris out of your gutters. We set up a landing page that offers a free 6-foot sample requiring that the customer just pay a low shipping cost, which separates the freebie seekers from the truly interested. Six feet is certainly not enough to offer total home gutter protection. Our intent is to follow-up with these free sample customers to upsell them into a 120+ foot package to protect their entire rain gutter system. The free sample offer is advertised on the web using Pay Per Click, video marketing, and through traditional methods such as radio shows, PR, television, and direct mail.

Here's what happens after someone requests a Free Sample.

a. Their contact information is transferred to our automated follow-up system. They will get an email thanking them for their request with instructions on how to test the sample product (We're teaching).

b. Three days later, we know they should have received the product by now, so the system will send them another email with installation instructions (Teaching again).

c. Now the system will send them an email every three weeks with further information about the virtues of gutter protection and our client's products (Teaching again and again), along with a unique coupon code they can use to buy more product.

d. They will also receive seasonally related messages throughout the year with coupon offers.

e. If they do come back and purchase more product, our automated follow-up system will remove them from the free trial campaign and place them into another follow-up campaign to seek referrals, reviews, and testimonials.

Apart from the initial setup and minimal maintenance by our staff, this automated program replaces the labor of several sales professionals, freeing sales pros to focus on much higher margin commercial accounts which, by the way, we integrate with automation as well.

2. Tracking

Digital integration also gives you a means of tracking the effectiveness of your direct response marketing campaigns. By directing people from your ad to a specific landing page, you can get a count of how many visited the page. You'll also get a count of how many people signed up to receive more information or perhaps used a unique coupon code mentioned in the ad. You can also track telephone calls, QR scans, and text messages.

This information is invaluable to your marketing campaign when properly executed and analyzed. Split testing advertising messages, as well as marketing channels, becomes easy. Plus, once you have enough data, you can not only determine how much exposure you received, but you can also determine how much each lead cost and whether or not the campaign was profitable. Over time, this information will help you better direct your ad budget, establish your bread and butter channels, as well as help you fine-tune your overall approach to marketing.

Track everything you do when it comes to marketing and advertising your business and services. The extra work will pay off dividends quickly.

Using marketing in a teaching manner establishes you as the go-to authority in your industry. It sets you apart and makes you a valuable resource to your prospective customers. Common approaches to marketing are the equivalent of saying, "Hey Customer, buy this service or product from me because I want you to give your money to me rather than my competitors." Digital integration will make your marketing "smarter" with each campaign.

About the Author

Carl Stearns is owner and principal consultant at Civic Mind Media, a digitally integrated full service marketing firm in business since 1999. Carl has helped A/E professionals, small businesses, consultants, doctors, veterinarians, coaches, government agencies and experts develop offline – online integrated businesses establishing themselves as thought leaders in their industry.

As a digital technologist combined with marketing expertise; Carl possesses a skillset rare in the industry. This combination of expertise and experience enables him to develop and execute marketing applications that significantly increase lead generation, sales conversion and online reputation without unnecessarily increasing marketing budget.

Carl and his firm have created well over 500 web sites, software applications and online training courses. His most recent success was to assist two retired veterinarians to transform their in-person classroom vet tech training business into an online training program increasing their total annual revenue 5x to a half million dollars while working from home.

Originally from Massachusetts, Carl, with his wife and two children, live in Coeur d'Alene, Idaho. He loves the resort community provided by Coeur d'Alene, the lakes and is an avid wakeboarder.

There's Money in This Book

> **Bonus Offer**: To receive a free Marcom Digital Integration checklist or to request a free marketing campaign analysis, please visit http://www.CivicMindedMedia.com/BookOffer

[1] "McDonald's spent more than $988 million on advertising in ..." Insert Name of Site in Italics. N.p., n.d. Web. 7 Aug. 2014 <http://www.csmonitor.com/Business/The-Bite/2014/0330/McDonald-s-spent-more-than-988-million-on-advertising-in-2013>.

Share Your Expertise: 5 Strategies for Creating an Engaging and Compelling Presentation
by Melodie Rush

Almost 20 years ago, I decided to change careers. I already had a soft job offer from a company waiting on a contract to come in when I got a call to interview for another job. I decided it would be a good experience to do the interview. So I interviewed with this company and when I returned home, I told my husband I really wanted that job. The only problem was that the next step in the interview process included doing a live presentation in front of people I would potentially be working with if I got the job. The thought running through my head was 'I'm presenting to the experts!' I was terrified, but I really wanted the job, so what was I to do?

One of their first requests was would I be using PowerPoint for my presentation. Now today that isn't an uncommon question, but back then I had not even heard of PowerPoint, much less had I used it. So of course, I said "Yes".

The weekend before the big presentation, I was struggling with what to present. I had taken a Public Speaking course in college, but nothing from that course really seemed to prepare me for the task at hand. I was almost in tears as I tried to organize the presentation. I then received some of the best advice on doing presentations that I have ever received and this was from my husband, who at the time presented on a regular basis to colleagues. He looked at me and said, "Tell a story." And I thought, *I can do that*. I proceeded to take the information I had put together and craft a story. I then put that story into PowerPoint. Fortunately for me, I'm a geek and a pretty quick study with software. With that said, I was still very nervous about presenting and remember my hands shook as I did my presentation.

Many research studies have found that the fear of public speaking is number one for most people (or at least in the top 10 greatest fears). There are many articles that address alleviating this fear. One of my favorites can be found on the Forbes website. The article is title "Five Reasons Why The Fear of Public Speaking Is Great For You". This article gives five reasons why you should speak in public. These include:

1. Be viewed as the leader
2. Increases Exposure
3. Gain Trust
4. Reduce Your Competition
5. Accomplish Something Great

After all isn't this what we aspire to do when we present our topic?

You can read the entire article online at http://www.forbes.com/sites/work-in-progress/2012/10/09/five-reasons-why-the-fear-of-public-speaking-is-great-for-you/

For this chapter, I want to help you minimize this fear by sharing with you 5 key strategies for creating a successful presentation. These include the following:

1. Identify your outcome
2. Determine the Audience
3. Prepare your content
4. Identify your props
5. Be yourself

Identify Your Outcome

Before you start, identify the outcome you hope to achieve. Are you teaching something? Are you selling a product or service (or yourself as I was doing in the interview)? Are you sharing an experience?

The most important thing for any presentation is to know what outcome you wish to achieve. For me, I usually share this outcome with the audience pretty early on by saying something like, "By the end of our time together, my goal for you is that you...." This way, I have set the expectations, both theirs and mine.

What do you want your audience to gain from your presentation? You need to establish a goal based on your outcome, so you know what and how to create the content. If you are teaching a concept, you will need to provide more details. If you are selling a product or service, you need to provide a value. If you are sharing an experience, you need to tell a story about an experience from your life.

Knowing the outcome helps you create a presentation to meet your goals!

Who is Your Audience?

The next step is to know who will be in your audience. Are they new to the subject matter or experts? If they are new, you will need to provide more background or intro information. If they are experts, you may be able to dive right into the subject. If you have a mixed audience, then you need to craft a message that will be relevant to all attendees. Now all attendees may be an impossible goal, but you can surely create a presentation that will be relevant to most of the attendees.

If you are an invited speaker, you will usually know who is attending because the coordinator will have that information and be able share it with you. Always ask the coordinator who will be there and what information they can give you about the people expected to attend.

If you don't know this information beforehand, you can always ask questions to the audience at the beginning of presentation. I usually do this, anyway, because sometimes the audience demographics have changed. Asking questions and having your audience participate is a great way to encourage engagement and get them involved.

Prepare your content

I cannot stress enough how import preparation is! Prepare and practice. Do not memorize your content; memorize the flow and let the words come naturally. Memorized word for word presentations are BORING! Off the cuff, poorly-prepared presentations are boring too and often hard to follow.

Early on I got the following advice to create presentations. It is still valid and still works.

1. Prepare an outline, usually 3-5 main points that you plan to share
2. Introduction – tell them what you are going to share with them
3. Body – tell them your 3-5 points
4. Conclusion – tell them what you have told them
5. Fill in 2-3 items you want to cover for each point
6. Practice your flow

More recently, I've updated this advice to include the following:

1. Prepare an outline, usually 3-5 points you plan to share
2. Come up with a story that will engage your audience. A personal story is most effective.
3. Weave the story throughout your points as much as possible, or
4. Tell mini stories to emphasis your points
5. And of course practice

By telling a story, you not only engage your audience, but you will make your points much more interesting. You will also better connect with your audience. I often tell an overarching story and insert shorter stories in the presentation. For example, weaving in other clients I have worked with not only builds my credibility, but also demonstrates my experience in the subject matter. And where appropriate I will tell stories of my mistakes or challenges. People like real people, not perfect people.

Identify your props

Props can make or break a presentation. You do not have to use props to be successful, but props can certainly enhance your presentation. The most common props used are slides; PowerPoint, Keynote, or Google Presentation. You can also use physical props. For example, Dave Ramsey, a popular financial guy, uses a big pair of scissors and a heavy chain with locks to help make his points on eliminating debt.

I have seen people use other props such as software that does mind mapping, videos, pictures, other people, audience participation, jokes, music, etc.

The key thing about props is to make sure they enhance your presentation and do not cause a distraction. Also make sure you practice with any props you plan to use. I've seen good props used poorly and it definitely creates a huge distraction.

One of my colleagues is a stand-up comedian in his spare time. I have seen his jokes be very effective in a presentation and I have seen them fall flat. I also like to use humor, but if I find my audience is not receptive, then I take on a more serious tone for the remainder of the presentation. What I mean by this is I will test the audience to see if my sense of humor connects with them. Most often it does, but once in a while not so much.

Slides are often the bane of many audience members. I have often heard people refer to daylong meetings as death by PowerPoint! Slides definitely can add or subtract from a presentation. Slides, if used, should emphasize what you are speaking about. They should not be used as a crutch for you to read, but only provide a nudge as to your next section of content. Or used to better illustrate a point you are making. Slides can provide great visuals to get your important points across to your audience. My best advice for slides is to keep them visual with pictures and images with minimal words.

Be yourself

Be authentic and you will attract the right people. When you try to be someone other than yourself, you will struggle to connect with the audience and you will struggle with your content. I've taken many public speaking courses and they have all fallen short on this one. All of the courses have taught a system or an outline for doing a presentation, but not one of them taught how to use that system with your own style (i.e., how to make it your own). I have learned a lot from these classes, but I have always left feeling like something was missing. And it was. In fact, I could often tell what course someone had taken when they presented. This is not good. It makes us all sound alike and in fact makes us boring. I am a constant learner, so I like learning new ways to do things. They key in presenting is to take what you learn and use it in your own style. This will insure the right people connect with you. You know connecting with your tribe is the most important thing you can do when you present!

So you may be wondering, did I get the job? Yes, I most certainly did. Confirming that the best advice I've ever gotten on doing presentations was from my husband and something you should remember and apply, "Tell a story".

Recently, I ran into one of the people that sat in on that presentation and she told me how impressed she was with my presentation. It turns out she was not technical and by me telling a story with the data and the technical output, she followed along without feeling confused (or stupid!).

Since switching careers, I have done over 1,000 live from stage presentations and well over 1,200 webinars. For sure my early presentations were not all glowing successes, but I have learned something from each and every one of them. In fact, the first few I did I was extremely nervous, but I took a big breath and got through them. I can tell you from my experience that it does get easier and in fact I really enjoy presenting.

Follow these five strategies and you will be well on your way to developing and delivering a successful presentation!

About the Author

Melodie Rush is a trained Statistician and holds a technical MBA. She has presented and consulted with many Fortune 500 companies, both domestically and internationally. Being a geek has not always been cool, but it has certainly given her the opportunity to teach and consult on many analytical topics across many industries. Her biggest strength is relating technical information to non-technical folks. She has an uncanny ability to simplify topics and chunk them into small bite-size pieces that even those afraid of technology can understand. Melodie is an experienced speaker both in person and via virtual webinars, having led more than 2000 presentations since 1996. She knows what works and what doesn't when it comes to doing presentations. She is the author of the soon-to-be-released book *Webinar Strategies*. Melodie launched We Create MVPs to share her knowledge and expertise by helping those new to doing presentations (either live or webinars) become powerful, influential presenters. Additionally, Melodie works with her clients to become recognized experts in their chosen niche through video, social media and online marketing. She most recently became an Instant Customer/Traffic Geyser coach and is a certified professional with Author Expert Marketing Machines. Her experience includes creating and implementing campaigns, surveys, analyzing data, and coordinating presentations, from 1 hour to 2 days. Melodie lives in Colorado with her husband and two cats. She loves to travel, scrapbook, and play with technology. In her spare time, she volunteers at the Denver Zoo as a Docent.

To download my 2 free bonuses:

1. "Establishing your Outcome Blueprint", a one-page worksheet to help you identify the outcome for your presentation

2. "The 10 Biggest Mistakes to Avoid when Creating Slides". This guide will help you avoid the most common mistakes people make when creating and utilizing slides in their presentations.

Visit www.melodierush.com/ShareYourExpertise or text your name and email address to 720-897-1999 or scan this QR Code

---

Keyword Research
by Jerry Dreessen

They really are just that – KEY words. They are the true key to any business online. Unless you are Coke, Amazon, Office Max or any other well-known brand, getting your message and product out there into the masses can be a make-or-break venture unless you possess... the KEY.

So what the heck IS a keyword? Well, it can be a single word or a 2-3-4-5-6 word phrase that people type into the search engines (Google, Yahoo, Bing) using a browser (Internet Explorer, Firefox, Safari) to find the products, services, or businesses and do commerce or education. Most people take all this for granted, but if you pull back the curtain, you'll see a very well-crafted campaign, purposefully designed by business owners to attract massive customers (or traffic) like Disneyland and families on vacation. And the having the best keywords for _your_ business will give you the best foundation for the Search Engines.

So here, without further ado, is my version of KEYWORD 101:

YOUR KEYWORDS MAY NOT BE WHAT OTHERS ARE SEARCHING FOR

First of all, are you a business, product, or service? Are you global, national, or local? Once you've got that figured out, the next question is who or what is your "Avatar"? An avatar is a rough to precise list/sketch/picture of your absolute best customer. An example would be if you sold doghouses, your avatar would be someone who has a dog that needs a doghouse. From that basic information, the path to proper keywords can begin. Coming from the healthcare industry, I have my set of descriptive words for my field. Unfortunately, they may not be the actual words my avatar is using to find me. For example, I may use the phrase "upper neck out of alignment" to describe one of my services, but my avatar may be online searching for "headache doctor". Unless I take the time to find out the exact phrases being used by my avatars, they will never find my website, and I'll just sit there in my clinic staring at all my degrees on the wall, wondering what went wrong.

There is also lingo you need to know regarding keywords. Once you understand this basic info, you'll be able to find the top keywords people are using to find YOU:

Synonyms: When you do a basic search, the search engines will return your key word/phrase with its artificial intelligence's best interpretation of what you want. Knowing all your synonyms for your product will also help you structure your keyword arsenal.

Short Chain/Short Tail: In the world of keywords, the short chain or 1-2 word phrases, are usually people (or avatars) looking for general information, unless it's for a product that is already known (Coke, Pepsi, etc.)

Long Chain/Long Tail: 3-4-5-6-7 word phrase. This is usually the phrase 'buyers' or 'key avatars' type in their search phrase. It means they've done their research and are ready to buy. An example would be "wooden dog houses for sale" or "easy to assemble dog houses" or "cheap wooden dog houses for sale". Usually this keyword phrase has some sort of "trigger to buy" synonym in it.

PPC Keywords: These are words used in a "pay per click" Adwords campaign. Adwords are those clickable advertisements you see on the top and to the right side in the search engines. Companies pay money each time someone "clicks" on their ad.

Broad Match: Keywords that contain all the words, but not necessarily in the right order. Example: "the **best** website for **dog houses**" and "**dog houses** made of wood are the **best**"

Phrase Match: Keywords that are part of a phrase, but maintain their order. Example: "**best dog houses** for sale" and "where can I find the **best dog houses** in Seattle"

Exact Match: Keywords that only contain the keyword. Ex: "**best dog houses**"; there are no variations.

Now that you have the basics, I want to walk you through how to do a basic keyword search using Google's "not so free" keyword planner. The reason I say this is because to use it for free, you have to create a Gmail account and an AdWords account. You'll need to create an ad campaign—but you don't need to make it active or spend any money. It just gives you access to their tool (It used to be free for anyone, but in 2013 they changed all that—I think they did it to regulate the amount of bandwidth that was getting used).

HOW TO DO A KEYWORD SEARCH

You can access the Google keyword planner from your AdWords account under the tools and analysis tab.

From the landing page, you can now select "search for keyword and ad group ideas" and enter your seed keyword just like the old Google keyword tool.

However, here is where it gets interesting. In the targeting options, you can now choose specific geo-targeting down to city, region, zip code or town. This is a huge improvement over the old keyword tool where you could only select by country. This makes the keyword planner perfect for local businesses who are wanting to discover keywords related to their catchment area.

Also in the targeting settings, you can choose whether you want keyword planner to return results just from Google or from Google and search partners. I strongly recommend that you choose "Google and search partners" because this is broadening the scope of keywords that get returned. By selecting "and search partners", Google will also be querying places like YouTube and the millions of search partner sites associated with it.

Now you can customize your search by setting keyword filters, e.g., only return results based on competition levels of high, medium or low. Obviously if you want it to return all results at all competition levels, tick all three boxes.

Finally, in the "include/exclude" settings, you can tell Google keyword planner to either include or exclude any certain search terms. This may be useful for example if you want to filter out search terms that may include the word "free" or "cheap" because you are not interested in optimizing for search terms including those words.

Now all you need to do is select "get ideas" and keyword planner will return results for you. By default, the results shown will be grouped into "ad group ideas". These ad groups are primarily for use on the AdWords platform, so simply select the tab labelled "keyword ideas" to get a list format.

Now you can start to filter through your keywords and analyze the data the keyword planner returns.

As I've mentioned, keyword planner is a major step forward in location targeting.

You should also be aware that the figures returned in keyword planner are exact match by default, unlike the old keyword tool that returned figures by default in broad match. You can of course change the match type by clicking the little pencil at the top right of the toolbar. However, you can only do this if you add keywords to the ad planner (which unless you're using the AdWords platform, you won't want to do).

The major downside to keyword planner is that it shows the results across "all platforms". That means that we can't differentiate between mobile searches and desktop searches.

Now that you have a moderate understanding of keywords, let's look at another way to study keywords:

Using the Search Bar: Ever notice when you begin to type in a search, just below the bar, "suggestions" are auto-populated for you? Usually the searches you've done show up, but down at the bottom of that, "suggested searches" also shows up. This is another "sneaky" way to scoop up keyword ideas that other people or avatars have typed in as well. Although you can't copy and paste them, you can leave your cursor over the area and take a screen shot to save them for later.

WAYS TO IMPLEMENT KEYWORDS

It's one thing to get a ton of great "avatar bait" keywords; it's another to know what to do with them.

If you are currently building a website, or have a webmaster who knows all about META tags, this section will help you transform your site so that the search engine bots will re-index your site for better rankings (incidentally, most websites get re-indexed every 16 to 18 days, unless you are constantly updating or adding to your site).

So how do you go about adding keywords to your site? Here are the major META tags, and how to best use them:

Title: This is the information that show up on the tab of the browser. Most people only have the word "home page" or "home". The title is shown at the top of your Google search return. Only the first 42 to 68 characters are visually displayed, and Google reads it as the first word having the most importance to the last word, which has the least importance.

For more in-depth information, refer to

https://support.google.com/webmasters/answer/79812?hl=en

To fully understand how your title and description look in the Google search engine returns, check out Doc Meyers Moz Blog, http://moz.com/blog/new-title-tag-guidelines-preview-tool. As you'll see, even using thin letters like "i" and "l" are better to use then "m" and "n" (and all caps) to get more characters in your search phrase.

Description: The description is based on a logical explanation of what your service or product is. However, you can stuff it with keywords and still make sense of it. Only stuffing keywords in it can trigger the indexers to rank you lower in the search results. A good example of a description would be "Find cheap and inexpensive wooden dog houses for sale. Dog houses are great for outdoor dogs". So in that phrase you can find all types of keyword combinations: "Cheap wooden dog houses for sale", "Inexpensive dog houses for outdoor dogs", "Outdoor dog houses for sale" – you can see that a longer description can pull different search results.

H1: This literally means, "The biggest, boldest header on the page" and is a key component for indexing. This is the keyword-rich phrase that is "shouting the loudest" on your site. If you are a blog writer, this is the header or title of your blog (which is why Wordpress blog sites are so popular).

H2: This is the 2nd largest, and often italicized, underlined, or a different color. It also stands out on your webpage and is indexed with more power.

Alt-tags: Alternate tagging is what you should do for all the pictures and images you have on your site. For example: "image1.jpg" is exactly how Google bots read the image. However, if you rename the image to "wooden dog house for sale", your site just jumped up one more rung in the search engines. A website with 5 or 6 images on the main page needs to take advantage of this. Even your logo needs to be something other than "main_logo.jpg" - change it to "Best Outdoor Dog Houses for Sale" or if you are lucky enough to have a business name that is keyword rich (hint hint) change your alt tag to that, e.g.: "Bob's Discount Dog Houses".

Hyperlinks or Anchor text: These are words on your site that, when clicked on, send you to a different link – preferably to a different page or section on your site. Again, the indexing robots assume that's important to you, and therefore important to them. Use your keywords for these hyperlinks as much as you can. Most of us just use "click here" (which you should have 1 or 2 of, but not all). If you are afraid your customers won't see them, or know they are supposed to click on them, simply state it like this: "For more information click on this link: Dog Houses For Sale" and make the keyword phrase the hyperlink.

Keywords: I put this last on the list, because this no longer carries the clout it used to. The awesome news is not a lot of webmaster or businesses know this and continue to load all 300 keywords in this section, which means you can "spy" on your competitor and see what keywords they are using for free, and not have to purchase spying software (although they do a better job at getting the best information).

LSI: LSI or "Latent Symantic Index" is a way to correlate semantically related terms that are latent in a collection of text. It's a technique of stuffing keyword phrases into sentences so that your site gets greater recognition in the search engines. A great resource to learn all about it can be found in this Wikipedia document:
en.wikipedia.org/wiki/Latent_semantic_indexing

That is the basic course for keywords. There are countless books on the subject if you want to advance to the "201" and "301" level courses. For some of you, this chapter is enough to get your site or project up and running. Which brings us to our next topic.

OK – NOW WHAT DO I DO?

This is a great question, and I am glad you asked it!

In order to get good search results for your website, you'll need to find out what type of competition already exists for your keywords. Your competition is based on other sites, how old they are, the number of backlinks, and a few other pieces of info that again is too much for this chapter to delve into.

Here's how I determine competition using free methods (I'll talk about paid methods at the end of the chapter): In the search bar, type in the keyword phrase that you want to rank for. After entering it and clicking the "search" button, you'll see below the field, "About XXXXX results (0.XX seconds)". That first number contains the number of BROAD MATCH results. Now put "" around the word. Notice the drop in number? This is the number of pages on the web that have these words in the exact order you wrote them. And now for my super-secret advanced technique that makes you glad you bought this book:

ALLINTITLE

If you put "Allintitle: KEYWORD" in the search field, you'll see the number of results drop even more. This gives you the true results of any website, article, etc. that are indexed exactly to that keyword phrase. Google will return all the sites it can find with all the words in the exact order you wrote them in. For example: "allintitle: green dog houses" will return roughly 1,710 results, vs 226 million results for Broad Match.

What does this mean? The lower the allintitle results, the easier it is for a brand new site to rank for. By putting all your keyword phrases in a "allintitle" search, you will begin to see which phrases are the easiest to rank for, and should start to build your site in that direction. If you have a blog site like Wordpress, you can begin to write posts and articles using those keywords as the title.

LOCAL VS NATIONAL

For those of you that are trying to get your product noticed in a local market, you'll find that all these numbers are a lot smaller. Sometimes ranking for these keywords is as simple as creating a page on your site with the keyword, because no one else has them!

What is a local set of keywords? A good example is a service industry: "San Diego Plumber" is one, "San Diego emergency plumber" is another, "San Diego Plummer 24 hour emergency plumber" is definitely a local specific niche. You can see how local keywords in combination with long chain keywords help local businesses rank better.

NICHE GENERATION – DRILL DOWN TO PERFECTION

Mike has a furniture business in Texas. He is in the process of building his website to attract local customers. Before buying his website and building it, he begins to do his "niche" homework, and drill down to the best "buyer" keyword triggers. So he grabs a piece of paper and in the center of it he writes "furniture". Next, he writes all the different main types of furniture around his main word, connecting them with lines. They are office, home, college, cottage, apartment, and lease to own. Now he focuses on only one of those subtypes – office. He writes out: reception chairs, desks, computer desks, cubicles – not just furniture he has, but also all the things a potential shopper might be looking for. As you can see, he has built a hierarchy from a general to a more specific list; he's "drilling down" to a more specific long chain keyword list. But it's still only based on Mike's knowledge. So the next step is to take those words and drop them into Google's keyword planner. Once Mike does that, he sees "desk chair", "work chair", "ergonomic work chair", "8 hour chair" "multi-lever chair" – all kinds of words and phrases real people are entering into the search engines to find office furniture to purchase. BUT to really see what keywords are popular and rising, Mike drops these keywords into another Google tool called "Google Trends". In that tool, he can see what phrases people are currently looking for.

After that search, he finds that "office desk furniture" is a trending word. So he takes that word, and types it into Google's search term and sees that as he types, the auto suggestion is giving him even MORE relevant search terms – up to 15 new terms. Mike did the same thing for all the other main branches of furniture. After about an hour – his list was complete.

His next step is to type in each phrase in Google, Bing, and Yahoo to see how many search results in the broad searches are returned. He types in "best Dallas Texas office chairs for sale" and looks at the results. He does that with all his top key terms. Now he knows how much competition each of his pages will have once they go live. Armed with that bit of knowledge, he now has groups of prime keywords to begin describing his avatar and designing his website.

On a separate sheet of paper, Mike draws a face in the center of the page. Surrounding the face he writes the words: "within 15 minutes to Dallas Texas, male and female, business owners, corporate businesses, college students and parents, have disposable income, shopping on a budget, joins an email membership site for special deals, seasonal repeat shopper, refers friends and other families, looks forward to seeing ads in the paper or online," etc. Now he has the "face" of his customer, and a target for his marketing. Next up, designing the website.

When building a website, each page built has its own page name that is used in the URL and the Title tag. For example, his website could be called; www.DallasTexasFurniture.com, and once a page is built and loaded, it becomes: www.DallasTexasFurniture.com/multi-lever-chairs-for-sale (other buyer intent keywords are: buy, discount, coupon, deal, etc. descriptor keywords are ones like: top, best, cheap, review, etc.). Here you need to be careful, because some websites/webmasters will build a site with pages having numbers and letters after them that the software assigns them – for example:

www.DallasTexasFurniture.com/as4ee90000978_pha45 – which will slow down ranking in the search engines.

Now you can see how a website can be built with combining local keywords with long chain keywords. Mike now adds pictures, with LSI keywords in the description of those images, and fills the entire page of "lever chairs" with trigger keywords that the search engines will help him rank for and bring his site to the first page of Google in Dallas, Texas.

Once Mike has drawn his website out on paper, he easily matches his inventory to each of the pages, and sends it all to his webmaster to begin building his site (or does it on his own using Wordpress eStore, Joomla, or a variety of easy-to-learn sites). Within days, Mike's site is up, and beginning to rank in the search engines for key buying words. The more content he can put in his website, the more Google loves him – and his website!

IS THERE AN EASIER WAY? YES. THERE'S ALWAYS AN EASIER WAY...

Now that you have a basic understanding (this is the 101 course, remember?) you can dig in even deeper to learn all about keywords, take what you just learned in this chapter, and go for it... or get a lot more information quickly with *PAID* services.

Paid services are applications you purchase and have on your computer that use the internet to give you all the results you need regarding keywords. With these paid services (some are one-time purchases, others are monthly) you can gain a huge advantage over your competition or gain a huge amount of information on how to begin ranking your product in the search engines in a shorter amount of time. Here are some paid services that I use in my personal business as well as for my clients:

Market Samurai for competition analysis with greater detail and depth FREE 5 DAY TRIAL:
   http://www.marketsamurai.com/c/WEBGUY11

Stealth Keyword Digger for local long tail
   http://www.stealthkeyworddigger.com/

Spyfu for keywords other businesses are using for organic and paid
   http://www.spyfu.com

Brad Callen's Niche Finder tool is great as well:
   http://082258ps-jxi9r22ys2-wokr5k.hop.clickbank.net/

Congratulations! You can now delve into the world of keywords and understand what people are talking about. I'm sure you are beginning to understand that ranking high in the search engines is no accident. Learning the terminology, performing searches for free, or utilizing paid services will help you grow your business online and will be looked on favorably in the search engine indexing systems. And now you know why keyword research is the core to a successful business online.

If you'd like to learn more about keywords and SEO for your business, you can sign up for my monthly email series by going here:
http://0s4.com/r/SEOKEY

About the Author

Jerry Dreessen has been in online marketing for over 10 years. He has read and studied multiple gurus on the subject of website construction, design, and Search Engine Optimization (SEO). He has implemented what he has studied to boost his online presence in his local market as a Chiropractor (videos, ebooks, landing pages), and founded his own company to provide website services as well. He is an Instant Customer Certified Consultant and has helped many people launch their business with the Done With You service. When he is not treating patients, designing websites, teaching or learning, he likes to hike and camp in the Pacific Northwest forests, and sail Hobie cats with his wife and 3 kids.

How To Create Profit-Pulling Sales Letters FAST... Even If You HATE Writing
by Steve Walther

If you want to double (even TRIPLE) the amount of money you make from your sales letters and online sales pages—even if you're brand new to copywriting or just flat out DESPISE it—then this chapter will show you how.

The following pages contain a simple, formulaic way to write ads and sales letters, learned over 13 years of trial and error creating marketing materials for myself and my clients as I collected and studied thousands of the most successful ads in history — from simple newspaper inserts that raked in $100 Million in sales over 100 years ago, to today's hyper-aggressive 7 and 8-figure internet product launches.

I'm going to give you my (very simple) 5-part framework to get inside the hearts and minds of your prospects, and predictably produce profit-pulling sales letters that sell. Your sales letter is one "leg" of the three-legged stool your promotion will sit on—the other two being your offer, and your list (or audience).

But before we dig in, a shameless bribe...

I'm looking for a "dream" client I can get massive results for.

If you're that client, I'd like to work with you side-by-side in your business to help you double, triple, or maybe even quadruple your revenue over the next 12 months.

You pay nothing out of pocket, ever... and here's why:

The first thing we'll do is create a strategic plan to bring you immediate profits. There's no charge for this and it only takes 30-45 minutes for us to strategize together.

I'll even do most of the heavy lifting for you... I'll help you figure out what to send, how to position your offer, find upsells, downsells, etc.

And at the end of this session, one of two things will happen:

1. You love the plan and decide to do everything on your own.

If that's the case, I'll wish you the best of luck and ask you to keep me posted on your progress.

2. You love the plan and ask to become my client so I can help you implement it.

When that happens, we'll knock it out of the park ...And that's a promise.

It really is that simple. There's no catch -- think about it:

The "worst" that can happen is you get a free plan to bring in immediate money just for "wasting" 30-45 minutes of your time.

On the flipside, we work together one on one to multiply your sales and profits many times over. You really can't lose.

Just shoot me an email at Steve@SteveWalther.com (my personal email address) and we can chat.

NOTE: That won't add you to an email list or sign you up for spam messages. That address goes directly to my email inbox, and I'll do my best to reply as soon as I can.

Alright—let's talk about sales letters...

The 5 Parts of a Successful Sales Letter

There are five distinct parts to most successful sales letters, and we'll cover each:

Part #1: Headline
Part #2: Lead or "Opener"
Part #3: Story
Part #4: Bullets
Part #5: Close or "Call To Action"

Let's dive right in.

Part #1: How To Create Headlines That Get Your Ads READ

Want to learn how to write "killer" headlines? Want a "super killer" or "ninja" trick?

Well, I've got bad news.

We don't care about writing headlines or ads that people think are "killer", "ninja", or "cool". The only feedback we care about is "I'm totally buying this."

That means only one type of headline will do—the kind that gets your sales letter READ. And the first step to making that happen is to figure out what your market really *wants* (and doesn't want).

This leads us to market research. Did you just say "yuck"? Look... I know it isn't a sexy topic. But if you want to write smashingly successful sales copy, there's no substitute for getting to know your market first, before you write a single word. In other words, skip this at your peril.

Get this right and you'll never write another limp, lifeless sales message ever again.

With enough research something magical happens. Your ad practically writes itself.

Gary Bencivenga (said to be the world's greatest living copywriter), once said that his mentor, John Caples, said the secret to successful copywriting is to gather EIGHT times more research than you think you'll need - on EVERY project.

With that much info on your market, you'll <u>NEVER</u> face "writer's block." You might have the opposite problem—figuring out what NOT to write!

So before you sit down to hammer out your headline, be sure you can answer these questions about your market:

- What keeps them AWAKE at night?
- What are their biggest FEARS?
- What causes them PAIN?
- What are their biggest FRUSTRATIONS?
- What HUMILIATES them?
- What makes them ANGRY?
- Who makes them FURIOUS?
- What do they WORRY about?
- What are their biggest VALUES?
- What is the biggest, most URGENT PROBLEM they face right now?
- Who is their common ENEMY?
- What is their average INCOME?
- What are their POLITICAL beliefs?
- What is their biggest DESIRE?
- What GROUPS do they belong to?
- What RELIGION are they?
- Is AGE, RACE, SEXUAL ORIENTATION, MARITAL STATUS, POSSESSIONS, OBSESSIONS, HOBBIES, or anything else relevant to how your product or solution can help them get the results they want?

This will get you focused on THEIR problems, instead of your product and its features.

Robert Collier (another old-school direct-response guy) was famous for saying "enter the conversation going on in your prospects' heads."

Here's the thing: if you can describe someone's problem BETTER than they can articulate it themselves... they'll assume you have the answer. And they'll grant you permission to help them with it (by giving you money).

Mess it up and watch your ad flop like a dead fish. Dale Carnegie said it another way, in How to Win Friends and Influence People:

"Personally I am very fond of strawberries and cream, but I have found that for some strange reason, fish prefer worms. So when I went fishing, I didn't think about what I wanted. I thought about what they wanted. I didn't bait the hook with strawberries and cream. Rather, I dangled a worm or grasshopper in front of the fish and said: '"Wouldn't you like to have that?'"

So step Numero Uno is to get in your prospects' heads and make sure you know what they want. Get to understand their problems... learn their language... talk like you're "one of them."

Then you need to figure out "what" to say. Here's two ways to come up with something useful:

The Stadium Pitch

This comes from Chet Holmes, the marketing and advertising manager for Charlie Munger (Warren Buffet's business partner in Berkshire Hathaway), and the guy that created the framework behind Anthony Robbins' "Business Mastery" program.

He calls it "The Stadium Pitch" in his book The Ultimate Sales Machine. In a nutshell:

Imagine a stadium filled with tens of thousands of your ideal prospects. You have 30 seconds to grab their attention... after that they're free to leave if they aren't interested in what you have to say. You step on stage, grab the microphone, and...

What comes out of your mouth?

The Knock-Knock

Imagine you're a door-to-door salesman in a rough neighborhood. Everyone has the problem your product can solve... but they HATE salesman, and they assume anyone knocking on their door is there to rob them.

"Knock-Knock" ...

The door opens wide enough for you to notice the barrel of a shotgun over the top of the security chain. What one sentence can you say to:

1. Stop them from IMMEDIATELY slamming the door in your face (or shooting you)... and...
2. Get them to invite you in, and ask you to tell them more?

Ponder those for a spell. When you think you've got "what" you want to say, let's look at a few proven ways for you to say it.

Headline Hacks

So the headline's only job is to grab a reader by the lapels and get them to read the next line of your sales letter... but how do we do that?

Just model what works. Don't worry, you'll get some exact examples of this in action in a moment.

My collection of über-successful ads (or "swipe file") goes back to the late 1800s. Many of those headlines (with very minor updates) are still being used successfully today. They're article titles and blog post names in The National Enquirer, Newsweek, and The Huffington Post... and can even be found working their magic as subject lines for campaign emails sent by the President of the United States.

Most of them are 50 years old, at least... originally written by direct response copywriting legends like Eugene Schwartz, John Caples, and Claude Hopkins.

Now I'm not saying you shouldn't be creative and try to "break the mold" if you know what you're doing... But if you're in a hurry, or just don't want to work that hard... or really just want the best chance of success right out of the gate - just model what works.

Here's how you can create your own formulas:

1. Take any great headline.
2. Distill it down to a fill-in-the-blanks "template."
3. Massage it to fit YOUR topic and industry.

For example, a proven headline like this:

"Arthritis Sufferers! Medical Doctor Discovers Deeply Hidden, Permanent, All NATURAL Solution That Gets Rid Of Arthritis After Only Two Weeks Of Treatment!"

Becomes a formula like this:

[Health-Problem] Sufferers! [Authority figure] Discovers Deeply Hidden, Permanent, All NATURAL Solution That Gets Rid of [Health Problem] After Only [Time Frame]!

And then "massage it" to fit your topic. Say you sell something for migraine headache sufferers...

Migraine Sufferers! Olympic Gymnast Coach Discovers Deeply Hidden, Permanent, All NATURAL Solution That Gets Rid of Migraine Pain After Only 15 Minutes Of Treatment!

Or something completely outside the health niche, like travel luggage. With a little tweaking, you might get:

Frustrated Flyers! After 1,000,000 Miles Of Air Travel, Airline Stewardess Discovers The Ultimate Solution To Packing Ultralight In 15 Minutes Or Less!

Not my best work, but you get the idea.

You can do this for book titles, blog posts, Facebook or other social media posts, email subject lines, article titles, video titles, ad headlines, whatever. Anything that needs an attention-grabber.

Below are 15 of my favorites.

Go through them and write 3 headlines using each formula. That gives you 45 headlines to choose from before you pick your winner.

You may want to dog-ear this page (or bookmark it if you're reading this on a Kindle) so you can get back to this page easily.

Fear Headlines

7 Warning Signs That [Blank]
Can We Really Trust [Person/Company/Product]?
13 Things Your [Trusted Person] Won't Tell You

Simple / Ease / Speed Headlines

The Zen Of [Blank]
The Minimalist's Guide To [Frustration]
11 Shortcuts For [Tedious Process] In Record Time

Mistakes Headlines

Do You Make These 13 Mistakes In [Blank]?
Don't Do These 5 Things When You [Blank]
11 [Blank] Mistakes You Probably Don't Know You're Making

How To Headlines

How To [Blank]
How To Be [Desirable Quality]
How To [Blank] (Even If [Common Obstacle])

Celebrity-By-Association Headlines

[Do Something] Like [Famous Person/Group]: 20 Ways To [Blank]
The [World-Class Example] School Of [Blank]
Secrets of [Famous Group]

... And a cool BONUS Formula

This comes from Dane Maxwell (creator of The Foundation):

[End Result Customer Wants] + [Specific Time Frame] + [Address The Objections]

In practice it would look like this:

"Land 5 New Clients Each Week Without Cold Calling or Rejection"

- or -

"Get Fit in 90 Days Without Diets or Exercise"

Ok... I'm not sure how that last one would work, but you get the idea. Happy Headlining, and don't forget to have fun along the way. When you're ready, we'll move on to...

Part #2: The 5 Sales Letter Leads That Make Cash Registers Sing

The "lead" or "opener" isn't as sexy as the headline, but it's the second most important part of your ad. Make it count. Here's a few proven formulas to get you past staring at the blank page.

The "If/Then" Lead

This is one of the most popular leads (and one of my favorites). It's easy to use, and wicked effective. Here's the formula:

"If you've ever wanted to [blank]... even if [objection]... then this might just be the most important message you ever read."

Here's an example:

"If you've ever wanted to write sales letters like a pro... even if you've never written one before and totally suck at writing... this might just be the most exciting message you'll ever read..."

If you go back to the beginning of this chapter, you can see how I used an "if/then" to start things off. Sneaky, eh?

The "If/Then + Authority" Lead

This is just like the last one, but adds a little authority "kick" for added credibility. Check it out:

"If you want to [blank] so you can [desire], [benefit], and [benefit], then here's how [authority group] does it... and how you can do the same with the information you're about to discover in this short message."

Here's a rough example:

"If you want to become a highly paid consultant so you can earn more money in less time, make a bigger impact with your message, and work from anywhere in the world... then here's how the world's highest paid internet copywriter does it... and how you can do the same with the simple system you're about to discover in this free training session..."

The "Open Loop Assault" Lead

Just hit the reader with a bunch of rapid-fire questions to pique their interest and pull them into your copy. They call unanswered questions an "open loop" in psychology-speak. For our purposes, we're just wrenching on their curiosity by stacking question after question. The right questions in front of the right audience are virtually impossible to ignore.

Here's an example aimed at consultants:

"Do you know why you should NEVER charge your clients by the hour? Or post your rates or packages on your website? Or ask prospects to schedule a meeting? In fact, these common, innocent

'mistakes' are probably costing you tens of thousands of dollars or more every year without you even knowing it..."

The Question Lead

This is similar to the above, but it's a single, simple, direct question about the target's needs, fears, or desires:

"Do you owe over $10,000 in back taxes to the IRS?"

"Got hemorrhoids?"

"Did you know that the long-term investment performance of Swarovski Crystal figurines outperforms most stocks, T-bills, and CDs?"

"If money were no object, would you drive this Rolls Royce?"

The Micro Lead

Simple. Effective. The "micro lead" starts small. Then the sentences get longer as the momentum picks up.
See how that works? You open up with a short statement that's easier to read than not read. Think of reading as "effort." Make it easy to start. Here's a few examples:

"POWER. I was impressed. I never thought that such a simple..."

"Never again. It was so embarrassing. I sat there, completely dumbstruck, wondering if..."

"Holy schnikes! Have you ever had such a great...?"

"Nasty. It was the only word I could think of. The entire room was gagging as he..."

The "Yes Set" Lead

This one's deceptively simple... and maybe a little sneaky, too.

It plays on this little psychological "hack" that exploits our lazy, pattern-seeking brains. Good salesman use this all the time in their presentations. Here's how it works:

Make two or more true statements, then follow it with a believable statement, and most people will assume that last thing you said is true... even if they can't really be sure if it is. It's like planting a thought in your reader's brain, *Inception*-style. Use it ethically. Statements are **bolded:**

> *"**You're here** because **you're interested in learning how to write better sales letters**, and if **my headline grabbed your attention**, then you probably already know why **you need to invest in my services**..."*

Tricky? Yes. Effective? You bet.

Part #3: Story-Selling

We're wired for story. It's in our DNA. Before written language, it was the only way to teach or learn ANYTHING. It's how we passed knowledge from caveman to cavewoman, huddled around the campfire. It's how today's world-class memory champs "hack" their memory capacity, and remember the order of multiple decks of cards—by assigning characteristics to each card and suit, then recalling the "story" to remember their order.

Want your marketing to have that kind of "stickiness?" Get good at telling stories.

There's about a ka-jillion different ways to do it, but I'll give you a simple one that consistently works like gangbusters. Yep... I said gangbusters.

"P-I-S-R"

Pisser: (US, slang) something special or outstanding; e.g. that story is a real pisser.

No, I didn't just go "potty mouth" on you. "P-I-S-R" stands for Problem - Implication - Solution - Result, and it's a powerful formula for connecting with your readers. Just one thing...

NEVER lie or make stuff up. The FTC will pimp-slap you (hard, with their ring hand), and your customers will run screaming for the hills. OK, maybe nothing quite so dramatic will happen, but still... people's BS meters are naturally on "red alert." So keep it real.

Here's an example of the PISR formula, using my own (true) story:

Problem

My name's Steve Walther. In 2001, I started my own consulting business. I had no experience, no idea how to market myself, and despite my optimism, things went bad VERY quickly. I spent all my savings on advertising that didn't work, and within a few months I was flat broke and frustrated.

Implications

It was the middle of winter in Chicago and I was two months late on my rent. My heat was shut off, my water was shut off, my 20-year-old rusted heap of a Jeep wouldn't start... and I had no money to fix any of those problems. I knew that if I didn't figure something out FAST, I'd wind up homeless. I really felt like I was at the end of my rope.

Solution

That's when I got serious about learning sales and marketing. I devoured every book I could find. Even when the money started coming in, I invested most of it right back in myself in the form of courses and coaching. I remember hearing someone say that "money buys speed", and that one idea changed my life. I made it a point to invest in learning from people that could save me the time and trouble of trial and error, and trying to do everything on my own.

Result

Within three years, I was landing five- and six-figure contracts with some of the biggest companies in America. I was in my mid 20's, and I was stealing A-list clients from guys with Harvard MBA's... and I never even went to college.

I was able to live and work right on the ocean in Biloxi, Mississippi for six months, and spent most of a year living in a luxury resort in the Caribbean. Most importantly, I created a simple system for delivering high-profit coaching and consulting services that let me work from anywhere.

As I refined my business, I went from working 18 hour days, 7 days a week, down to just 15 to 30 hours a week... all while getting better results for my clients, raising my rates, and increasing my income, year after year.

Recap of the "PISR" Story Model

From there you could transition into "And now I'm looking for a few clients to join me in an exclusive program where I'll be teaching you exactly how to do it, even if, like me, you're just starting out and have no experience or credentials as a consultant. You'll discover:"

And BOOM! That take us right into the bullets, then the close.

So sit down and think about YOUR story, or the story of someone your product has helped (or is designed to help). What problems did you face? What would have happened if you didn't fix those problems? What discovery or solution saved you from the brink of destruction? What was the end result?

Make sure you always end on a high note! People invest when they're inspired—and usually don't when they're depressed.

Got it? Cool. Now let's move on to...

Part #4: Bullets

What are bullets? These are bullets:

- This is a bullet.
- This is a second, even cooler bullet.
- And this is a third, most impressive bullet (with extra stuff in parenthesis)

Bullets are a powerful part of your sales letter. They're easy on the eyes, and an easy-to-digest way to present information. Our eyes are drawn to them, and our brains LOVE them. Ben Settle, a world-class email copywriter, says "there's a reason we create grocery lists, and not grocery paragraphs." True, true.

But there's a bit of a science to creating bullets that sell. A grocery list is about straight information, but sales page bullets need to tease people.

Tease people? Isn't that just mean?

It seems weird, but think about it. People like to be teased. It's why casinos and strip clubs are so profitable.

John Carlton teaches what he calls "blind bullets"—teasers that grab hold of your curiosity glands and SQUEEZE so hard you almost have to buy (without ever giving you ANY hard information). Master the blind bullet, and prosper.

Here's a few examples of bullets "selling" this chapter:

- The 5 "magic parts" of highly profitable sales letters (and over 20 easy-to-use "templates" for banging them out at lightning speed!)
- 15 user-friendly "headline hacks" to easily create attention-grabbing titles at-will—for anything! (Ads, book titles, blog posts, email subjects, and more!)
- The little-known "Story-Selling" formula that creates instant rapport with virtually any audience!
- 5 easy-to-use "templates" for starting your sales letters so you magnetically PULL readers deep into your copy!
- How to BANISH writer's block FOREVER with this one simple trick (the same trick used by two of the greatest copywriters who ever lived)! Do this right and you'll have so many ideas you'll need to worry about what NOT to write!
- … And 5 sales letter closing strategies you can use in your sales letters TODAY (combine them all and MULTIPLY your chances of closing the sale!)

Those are a bit rough, but you get the point. They grab your attention with curiosity, and there's no immediate payoff. You have to buy the book (or read this chapter) to find out what the bullets are talking about.

Now grab a piece of paper and come up with as many bullets as you can. Be outlandish. Don't censor yourself… just write. Then go back and pick the winners, and clean things up as needed.

"Write drunk, and edit sober."—I think Hemingway said that.

Anywho… from the bullets, you can just slide right into…

The "Close" or "Call To Action"

This is the most exciting part—where you ask for the sale and GET THE MONEY (if you do it right). Below are the 5 parts of successful sales letter closes. Use them all, or mix and match until you find the right combination for your market and offer.

1. The Transition
2. The Guarantee
3. Fast-Action Bonuses
4. The Takeaway
5. The P.S.

The Close Part #1: The Transition

This, plain and simple, is a sentence or phrase you use to smoothly move from "here's what I got" to "here's what I want you to do now." And really it can be as simple as that. Here's a few more examples:

"So here's what I'm offering."

"Here's how you can get in on this."

"Alright... here's the deal:"

Then just give them the price and tell them how to order, or flow straight into one (or all) of these other 4 sections.

The Close Part #2: The Guarantee

Most of the time, having a guarantee helps sales... but not always. It depends on your positioning. Think about Donald

Trump. He doesn't need to offer a guarantee... He's "The Donald."

Assuming you're NOT currently an angry billionaire with an even angrier comb-over, you'll probably want to include some kind of guarantee to set your prospects' minds at ease. That could be a money back guarantee, the "it works or it's free" guarantee, or even "double your money back" if you're confident about your product.

Think like your prospect. What would make your offer a complete no-brainer? Like the mechanic that says "if this doesn't fix your car, I'll buy it from you outright." Or the martial arts school that says "try our classes, and if you hate them, I'll pay for 3 months of your lessons at any other school of your choice."

When possible, do what you can to make your offer a no-brainer.

And here's a tip:

It's a bit counterintuitive, but the LONGER your guarantee period is (30 day, 90 day, 90 year, Lifetime, whatever), the FEWER people will actually take advantage of it. Test it for yourself and see.

The Close Part #3: Fast-Action Bonuses

You don't have to have them, but more often than not, a good bonus will knock a few extra people off the fence. Sometimes they buy just for the bonuses (I've done that more than once).

Here's how you might do it:

"And if you're one of the first 5 people to invest in this course, I'd like to offer you a special added bonus."

Then just tell them what they get. It could be a call with you, a recording of an interview you've done, access to some resource that will help them... whatever makes the deal irresistible.

Frank Kern, another one of my mentors, calls it "stacking the cool." He keeps adding cool bonuses until you can't take it anymore and hit the buy button. Not a bad way to do it...

The Close Part #4: The Takeaway

I use this one pretty often, mostly because I want to repel people who aren't a good fit for what I'm selling. It works extremely well with big-ticket purchases. (I've seen it used successfully to sell real estate and luxury vehicles as well.)

You need a tough mindset to pull this off though. And you have to be OK with telling people like it is (and pissing a few of them off). Here's an example of what I'm talking about:

"This offer is NOT for everyone. It's **very** expensive, and once you apply, there's no guarantee you'll be accepted. I need to interview you to see if you're a good fit, and most people don't make the cut. Because of the demand and limited number of spaces available, if you want in on this, you have to be a fast action taker, and an implementer."

Here's another:

"If you're offended by occasional profanity, or can't handle unfiltered feedback about your marketing (followed by no-BS advice on how to fix it), chances are we're not going to work well together. I don't have time to candy-coat the truth for you, and you shouldn't want me to. There are plenty of other consultants that will do that for you, but you won't get that from me. If what I said offends you, I understand—and respectfully ask you not to waste my time (or yours) by signing up for this course, only to have me eject you later."

Kinda aggressive, right? But effective.

Almost nobody has the guts to put themselves out there like that, and when you do you, stand out like a loud fart in church. More importantly it pushes away people you don't want as clients anyway, and gets people that might have been whiners to "toughen up"... making your life easier in the long run.

The Close Part #5: The P.S.

If you listen to the old-school direct response guys (the ones that make millions selling stuff through the mail), they'll tell you the P.S. is the most read part of any sales letter next to the headline. Maybe so. On a sales page, I think the equivalent is the bottom of the page, where the price and offer usually are. People read the headline, skim the bullets, and scroll right down to the bottom looking for the process... which makes it a great place to include testimonials, an offer recap, a list of bonuses, a countdown timer or deadline, a takeaway, etc.

And that, for now, is a wrap on sales letters.

Final Thought

Test, test, test.

You never REALLY know what works best for your offer and your list until you TEST. Try different things… experience will be your best teacher. This chapter is just a "jumping off" point.

> And of course, another shameless plug—If you want FREE feedback on your stuff, or want to explore working together in the future, just drop me a line: Steve@SteveWalther.com.

Thanks, and good luck!

—Steve Walther

Video Marketing
by Sandi Masori, CBA CMT.

We know that the online marketing game has changed a lot in the past few years. One of the most solid and search-engine friendly ways to market online is with videos.

Why is this approach so powerful you may wonder? Well, the reason is that the search engines are always looking for the freshest, most relevant information to return in a query, and often videos provide just that. Also, YouTube, which is owned by Google, is the second largest search engine, after Google itself.

That means that people are going to video sites like You Tube to find out information. People like to watch videos. Especially short ones. So, when they start looking for something, your video could show up in the search results in Google and/or in You Tube (and the other search engines as well). Besides that, the strength of YouTube video itself means that there are huge SEO benefits from the resulting link. *(Translation, links on YouTube video descriptions = Google love for website.)*

Often when I talk to clients about video marketing, they start telling me about how they did a couple of web commercials and it was really expensive and didn't really get them anywhere. When I hear that, I can't help but think, "well, duh."

While it's a great idea to have a commercial, or a sizzle reel on your website, no one is going to go looking for it. The key to video marketing can be summed up as, "What are people looking for" as it pertains to your niche. That's what you should be making videos on.

One of my mentors recommends sitting down and writing 20 questions about your business. The first 10 questions should be frequently asked questions (FAQ) and the second 10 questions should be "should ask questions" (SAQ).

These questions should be about your business or niche. So the question "Why are you better than the guy down the street?" is not a good FAQ question. Let me give you an example from the balloon industry. One of the most frequently asked questions of balloons (in the search engines) is "What is the fear of balloons called?" Since people are looking for this, and typing it in, this could be a great question to do an FAQ video on. A great SAQ question might be "What are the California Balloon Laws?" This is also an important question about the niche, but refers to something that people may not even know enough about to ask.

Let's pretend that we have a blue widget factory. A good question might be, "What makes a good blue widget?" So right now, take a moment and write out your list of 20 questions.

Each one of those questions is the title of a video.

When you shoot the video, be sure to first give the question, and then just answer it. Don't write your answer down or try to read it; just talk to the camera. You know this stuff, you're an expert, so just talk.

That's really the whole point to all of this—you want to give your prospects the chance to know, like, and trust you. If you are reading from cards or not looking at the camera, you won't be able to make that connection with the viewer.

For many people, it helps them to have someone behind the camera who asks them the question. In that case, make sure that you restate the question as part of your answer, just like you may remember from the SATs. The length of the video should be as long as it needs to be to get the point across and no longer. Ideally it should be around 1-3 minutes, but no longer than 5, unless absolutely necessary. People have very short attention spans.

17 Secrets from a Marketing Mastermind

One of the objections that I hear from clients who are new to video marketing is that if they are just giving away information, how will that help them make more sales? That is achieved by the call to action at the end of the video. After you answer the question, there should be some sort of offer, for example "For a FREE e-Book, come to www.MyDomain.com". This single slide has the call to action, or the ad.

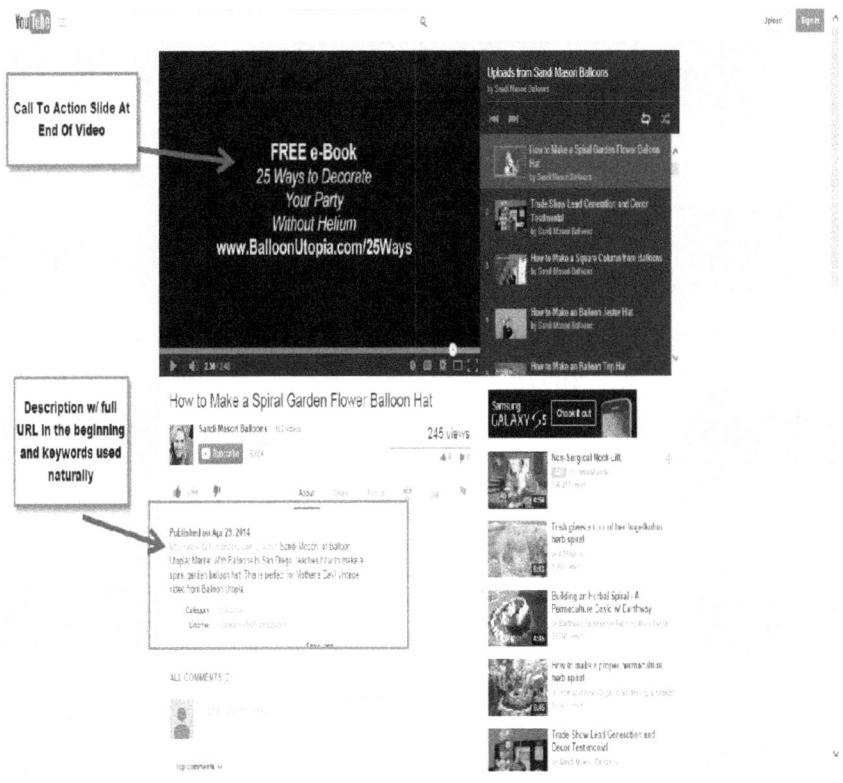

Ideally, you want the call to action to get them onto a marketing list so that you can sell to them later. There are many different things that you could offer your prospects. You could invite them to get an e-book, as in our example above; you could offer a discount; a buy-one, get one; a video series;

enter a contest; get a free report, etc. The call to action needs to resonate with your audience and offer them an answer to their problem.

Personally, I have found that an e-book works best for my audience, as well as for the audiences of many of my clients. You may need to play with it to find out what would work best for you, however.

In my experience, there are three reasons why a video may not convert. They are:

1. Nobody is looking for your video
2. The video is boring, doesn't resonate, or is hard to hear
3. The call to action doesn't resonate with your audience

Let's address these issue one at a time. If the problem is that no one is looking for your video, then go back and look at the title. Is the title of the video a question? Are you using industry specific words or jargon? Does it offer an answer to a problem?

Go back to your keyword research and figure out what word people are typing in when they ask the questions. For example, doctors love to use medical terms, but likely people aren't googling "Why do I have acute abdominal pain?" They're probably typing in: "Why does my tummy hurt?"

If you're not sure, then go to Google and start typing in the question, and pay attention to the suggestions that Google makes as it tries to intuit what you may be asking.

17 Secrets from a Marketing Mastermind

```
why does my |
why does my eye twitch
why does my stomach hurt
why does my lower back hurt
why does my cat bite me
why does my jaw hurt
why does my dog eat poop
why does my chest hurt
why does my throat hurt
why does my dog eat grass
why does my knee hurt

        Google Search    I'm Feeling Lucky
```

If the problem is that you don't resonate with your audience, then you may need to work on your camera presence. How is your energy? You need a lot of energy to be on camera. If you are a low energy person, then do something, like bouncing, to up your energy before going on camera.

I already mentioned the trick of having a friend behind the camera. Another trick is to imagine that you are explaining the answer to the question to your favorite aunt.

If you still find yourself being awkward on camera, start keeping a daily video journal. Every day, take out your smartphone and make a little video. It doesn't matter what it's about, and you don't have to post it anywhere, but if you do it every day, you will find yourself feeling much more confident on film.

You could also do a slideshow video with a voice-over, using either your voice or a professional actor, but my personal opinion is that it's much stronger to appear on camera yourself.

After all, our goal is to let people get to know, like, and trust you. So, let them see you and your knowledge and passion.

If the problem is bad sound, or background noise, or static, then you're best off making a whole new video. People will put up with a lot regarding the quality of the video, but nothing will make them hit the close button faster than bad audio.

And lastly, the reason that the video is not converting to leads may be because of the call to action or the offer. If it's not resonating with your audience, then try a different one.

In some ways, getting the call to action right is like cooking spaghetti. Sometimes you just have to throw it against the wall and see what sticks.

At the time of this writing, my channel (http://www.YouTube.com/Sandiballoon) has 180 videos, over 7,000 subscribers, and over 1.7 million views. If you look through my videos, you'll see how I played with my call to action. First I tried offering a discount, but that didn't do much. Then I tried a contest, and that was a little better, but still didn't yield the results I had hoped for. Finally I put up an e-book. In just a few months, that book has collected over 1,200 opt-ins. So that is what resonated the most with my audience.

If you create your video marketing strategy so that you are looking at a long-term plan of putting out a video a week, every week, then you have plenty of opportunity to play with the offer.

Now that you've made all of these videos, what should you do with them?

I recommend using a video syndication system to put them out in multiple places all over the internet. That way, you can shoot all the videos in one day, schedule them to go out once a week for the next few months, and then forget about it for a while. You'll love how easily leads pour in once you figure out your audience and offer, and settle into a rhythm.

> Do you need help with your video marketing? Contact me at Sandi@webcoach4you.com

About the Author

Sandi Masori, CBA CMT, is a two-time best-selling author, TV personality, coach, marketer, and balloon expert, (and a mom, daughter, and wife). She began her journey into online marketing in 2008 when she wanted to upgrade the Balloon Utopia website and improve her position online.

Masori initially took a "marketing boot camp" class from a fellow balloon artist, and then went on to learn from the teachers he mentioned throughout the course. She found the nuances of the marketing ecosystem fascinating and continued taking higher level courses on the subject. Along the way, she found herself helping others with their marketing and in 2010, she took her first of many certification courses to become a marketing technologist and coach.

Masori began coaching other business owners on how to take control of their own marketing through her WebCoach4You site. She also realized, while working with her corporate clients on the balloon business, that she was often being asked to help with some aspect of the event marketing. A light bulb went off and she began to incorporate both balloons and marketing into her corporate business. Market With Balloons (Http://www.MarketWithBalloons.com) was born. She authored and published the best-selling books *The Ultimate Guide To Inflating Your Tradeshow Profits.... With Balloons* and *The Event Planner's Essential Guide To Balloons*.

There's Money in This Book

She has produced hundreds of marketing videos, for both her own channel and those of her clients. At the time of this writing, Sandi's YouTube channel, *Sandi Masori Balloons* (http://www.youtube.com/sandiballoon) has almost 7,000 subscribers and 1.7 million views. She has appeared on local and national TV shows like *Daytime* and *The Today Show*. She was quoted as saying, "Everything I learn I try to apply to my own business first, and if it works, then I can I teach it, or do it for others."

Mobile Devices and Marketing
By Steve Laurvick

There is no questioning the fact that mobile marketing strategy must be a primary consideration for every online advertising campaign, and every new and existing website. Bear in mind, however, that while there is a great deal of traffic to be acquired by building mobile device friendly websites, there are also misconceptions about which products and services will convert into leads and sales. The famous line by James Earl Jones in *Field of Dreams,* "If you build it, they will come," is actually true if you do the work and optimize your campaigns for both search engines and mobile devices, but that doesn't mean they will buy when they land on your sales page. It also means you need to consider whether or not to spend advertising dollars on mobile applications or venues.

Let me share some sobering statics from a recent study by Pew Research.

As of January 2014:

- 90% of American adults have a cell phone
- **58% of American adults have a smartphone**
- 32% of American adults own an e-reader
- 42% of American adults own a tablet computer

(For current statistics, click on or copy and paste the link below into your browser: http://www.pewinternet.org/fact-sheets/mobile-technology-fact-sheet/)

As of this writing, nearly 60% of adults in the USA have a smartphone, and that smartphone will never be more than 10 feet away from the owner for the rest of their lives. It is not only the consumer's primary way of communicating with friends and family, it is also the mobile device user's lifeline for solving everyday problems.

NEWS ALERT: *July 17, 2014* IBM and Apple have signed an agreement to bring IOS applications to the enterprise marketplace. A new IBM website boasts, "A new generation of mobile enterprise solutions combines the power and ease of use of iOS with IBM's industry knowledge, consulting, and delivery services." The partnership between the once rival computing solutions giants means that iPhones and iPads that had been relegated to consumer use will now enter the corporate world. Apple and IBM will build cloud based solutions that will put mobile devices into the hands of hundreds-of-thousands of employees worldwide, "The IBM MobileFirst Platform provides an enterprise-class cloud solution for building and deploying elegant, integrated apps for iOS."

What does it mean?

It means that mobile device ownership and use is about to become ubiquitous. In a very short time, virtually anyone who you would like to sell your businesses products and services to will be using mobile devices on a regular basis.

So let's get down to brass tacks on this vital piece of your business planning.

There are four key elements of mobile marketing currently being taught by experts, by people calling themselves experts, and by mobile marketing product vendors like Apple and Google.

1. **Paid mobile traffic.** A lot of the mobile marketing products out there actually have nothing to do with free traffic because what they are really teaching is how to get paid mobile traffic using ad networks such as AdMob, which is owned by Google and InMobi.

A little history: When these mobile ad networks were first made available to the public, it was similar to the Google AdWords launch in 2005. There was very little competition among AdWords users and it was easy to get cheap traffic and send it anywhere. That is no longer the case with AdWords. Today, it is more competitive and increasingly there are more rules and restrictions. There are still great opportunities and still a massive source of web traffic to tap into, but the person involved has to treat it just like any source of paid web traffic.

Today, the marketer has to become a paid traffic expert; otherwise, a lot of money will be left on the table. Clearly, risk is involved, but those who become experts at getting paid web traffic will make a lot of money either for themselves, their clients, or both. This is because they have mastered the process of turning nickels, dimes, and quarters into dollar bills. Business owners who foray into the minefield of pay-per-click (ppc), cost-per-acquisition (cpa), and other online advertising methods need to prepare themselves for a tedious, time-consuming and potentially expensive learning curve. A good online advertising company is worth its weight in gold to a business owner.

There are currently hundreds of mobile advertising networks that have jumped into the business and are competing for advertising dollars. As this market becomes more mature, this number will eventually decrease, as the biggest players will eventually kill off and absorb the small networks. In the meantime, there are definitely opportunities to be explored.

The largest ad networks generally have the ability to deliver the highest volume of traffic, but the smaller networks often have less competition. Some of the networks to check out are Google Mobile Ads at AdMob.com (which is now a part of the AdWords program), Apple's iAd network, InMobi, Jumptap, Millennial Media, adfonic, BuzzCity and MobPartner. MobPartner is an interesting one because it is actually a mobile affiliate network; basically like a CPA network. Instead of paying per click or paying per one thousand impressions, the marketer pays per action. This means that he only has to pay when he gets a lead or a sale.

2. Mobile applications like iPhone and Android apps. Mobile apps are a great way to make money. They are potentially one of the most profitable types of digital products that anyone can sell because there is such a huge market for them. They can also be a great way to get web traffic. Many mobile apps are used as a means of accessing the Internet. For example, rather than constantly visiting a webpage to check the weather, a lot of people use a weather app. The same principle is used for all sorts of websites. For example, I could create an Oracular Marketing app that gives daily tips and charge for it or give it away for free if someone gives up their name and email address and becomes a subscriber on my list.

There are many ways to have a mobile app created. Obviously, programmers will have an easy time creating their own apps. For those who are not, they can simply outsource it. The amount to be paid depends on what the person needs. For instance, an average iPhone app costs anywhere from hundreds to thousands of dollars. Obviously, just like a piece of software or website, if it would be a really complex app, then the person would need to spend tens of thousands of dollars. But, if it is something very simple, it can be created with only a budget of five dollars. There are several programmers offering their services on Fiverr and they will create a unique iPhone app for only five dollars. The app has basic features such as logo of the company or business, some pictures, a quick dial button, links to the business' social media, map of the business' location, a short write up about the app, and much more. More importantly, this app can be sent to friends or contacts via SMS or email. No iTunes required. It's that simple.

A more professional way of creating apps is through Seattle Clouds, available at http://oracularmarketing.com/seattlecloud. They have a web-based app builder that will allow one to quickly build an iPhone app or an Android app. Unlike with Fiverr, Seattle Clouds will submit the created app to iTunes or to the Android marketplace. They also have the option of setting up a monthly membership or lifetime pre-paid fee for one app, a package of apps, or a business brand less previewer with unlimited apps. And they guarantee that your new apps will be approved and if not, you get your money back. Their price starts at only ten dollars a month.

Appmakr.com is another way to create an app. It is a free application, but there will be pop-up ads on it. Appsmakerstore.com is a similar product with a basic free plan with restrictions on the number of visitors per month. Testing is always necessary in online marketing, so using the free plan until you create a campaign achieving your results can do no harm. You could then upgrade to the premium plan for an unlimited number of visitors. As of the date of this writing, they have a nine-dollar per month plan or the marketer has to pay a premium price of forty-nine dollars a month.

Aside from iTunes and Android marketplaces, some additional places for marketers to list their apps include GetJar.com, Handster.com, appslib.com, (only for Android tablet apps), and Amazon Appstore for Android apps.

3. **SMS Marketing.** SMS stands for Short Message Service, better known simply as text messaging. SMS text is an under-used marketing tool and a double-edged sword. A lot of people actually refer to this as mobile marketing. So when they talk about mobile marketing, they are actually talking about SMS Marketing, when in reality it is simply one method of mobile marketing.

According to one SMS marketing site, the average text message is read within three minutes. This alone makes it a great way to communicate with prospects and subscribers.

Obviously, due to the format, it is much more limited than email – for example – because the message has to be kept short.

How does it work?

One of the more common ways to do it is through message like this: "Text X, Y, and Z to such and such numbers to receive your free coupon." This is a mobile opt-in system. Once a person sends a text to that number, he is added to the list. Sometimes there is a double opt-in system where the person who sent a reply has to confirm his subscription by replying to their confirmation text. It is very similar to the way an email opt-in list works, except for the fact that mobile messages are much, much shorter.

What kind of SMS to send? Text them coupons and special deals that they are going to find valuable. For affiliate marketers, find products that they would be most interested in and promote those products to the SMS list. Those offers can be found on CPA networks or affiliate program providers like ClickBank. It goes without saying that the more targeted your list is, the better. Brick-and-mortar businesses are benefiting from SMS marketing just as much as online businesses, so for a local marketing consultant, this is something that he should definitely be incorporating into the services he is offering. One way to make money is to become an affiliate or a reseller of an SMS marketing provider. When clients sign up, the affiliate marketer gets money.

There are also several SMS marketing companies that offer white label reseller programs wherein affiliate marketers can sell to their clients under their own brand names. These providers include mobilesmsmarketing.com, textsmarks.com, trumpia.com, avidmobile.com and callfire.com.

How much does SMS marketing cost? First, it is not free. The marketer has to pay for every message sent. Over time, the price has gone down and will probably continue to go down. But right now, it costs anywhere from about one cent to twenty cents per message, which is a pretty big range. Those who want their own short codes normally require several thousand dollars a month on top of the messaging fees. On the cheaper end of the spectrum at one cent per message, there is Twilio, which is sort of a self-serve platform. A WordPress plug-in, WordPress VBX, makes it easy to use Twilio. Check it out at chadwyatt.com/wpvbx.

MMS (Multimedia Messaging Service) marketing is very similar to SMS marketing, with the difference in the fact that there is an embedded media in the text message being sent. As technology continues to improve, these two forms of marketing will probably merge into one.

Proximity marketing is a bit of a different beast altogether and it is not commonly used by Internet marketers at this time. The way it works is advertising messages are transmitted to mobile device users who are physically within a certain area. For example: Someone can be walking down a sidewalk and then walk by a restaurant. Just as this person is walking by the restaurant, a coupon for that restaurant is beamed to his mobile phone and magically appears on it. There are all kinds of information that can be distributed through proximity marketing, but since it is generally done in conjunction with something in the real world, it is best utilized by offline marketers rather than Internet marketers.

SMS has been around for over 20 years, and has grown to become the king of communication in the US and UK, surpassing phone calls and even face-to-face communication. The statistics we've compiled below prove just how popular SMS is, and why brands should start exploring the world of SMS to enhance customer experience, increase sales, and improve customer service.

BEWARE OF STATISTICS ABOUT SMS:

More than any other form of marketing, text messaging is personal.

Don't believe me?
- The average person looks at his/her phone **150** times per day (Nokia)
- **59%** of single people approve of breaking up a causal relationship via SMS (Spark Networks)

...And 24% say breaking up a *serious relationship* via a text message is ok!

Here's the deal, statistics don't lie; people who use statistics to sell you stuff lie.

Here are a bunch of stats about SMS text messaging I just pulled up online:
- 80% of consumers say they have not been marketed to via SMS by their favorite brands (Hipcricket)
- 57% of consumers say they would be interested in opting into a brand's SMS loyalty program (Hipcricket)
- 90% of mobile users who participated in an SMS loyalty program felt they had gained value from it (Hipcricket)

80% of consumers haven't been marketed to via SMS because 80% of cell phone users are very reluctant to give out their cell phone number to anyone they don't know. Most of the remaining 20% are receiving text messages from a company because they bought something from the company and they were willing to give up their cell number because they liked the product.

2. SMS Marketing campaigns are opted out of less than 5% of the time (Slick Text)

Most of the consumers on the receiving end of an SMS Text marketing campaign have already received something they like from the sender and they trust them. But again, very few people are willing to give up the phone number without a really good reason.

3. SMS Marketing coupons are 10x more likely to be redeemed and shared than mail or newspaper coupons (Slick Text)

I think you would agree that it would seem pretty hard to "share" a newspaper or mailer coupon, while it is simply a matter of forwarding an online or text coupon. It is also much easier to carry a digital coupon than to snip it out of the newspaper and remember to bring it to the grocery store.

4. 70% of people in the US would like to receive offers on their mobile phones (Upstream)

I am skeptical here. I think you would agree with me that it would depend on what type and how many offers one would really want per hour or day. The point here is not that you shouldn't be using SMS texting in your campaigns—in fact, quite the opposite. The point is you need to be very careful about how and how often you use text messages in your campaigns. The first time you violate the trust of the customer who deigned to give you his/her cell phone number is very likely to be the last time you will send him/her a text message because they will opt out.

Secondly, you need to carefully consider asking for a cell phone number on a standard squeeze page or opt-in form. The purpose of an opt-in form is to make it easy for someone to put themselves on your list. The moment someone sees an opt-in box asking for or requiring a cell phone number (or phone number period), the less likely they will be to fill out the form at all.

I'll finish this section with more statistics for your perusal:
- 75% (4.5bn) of the mobile phones worldwide are SMS enabled
- 150 billion text messages were sent in the UK in 2011 (Ofcom)
- 96% of smartphone users use SMS (Acision) tweet this
- The average UK consumer sends around 50 text messages a week (Ofcom)
- Text messages are read on average within 5 seconds (Frost & Sullivan)
- The average delivery time for SMS messages is under 7 seconds (Simply Cast)
- SMS is the most popular form of communication in the UK (Ofcom)
- SMS produces engagement rates 6 to 8 times higher than email (Cellit)
- 98% of text messages are read, compared to 22% of emails, 29% of tweets and 12% of Facebook posts. (Frost & Sullivan 2010, Slick Text)
- The average click through rate (CTR) of URLs included in SMS messages is 19%, compared to just 4.2% CTR for emails (TextBoard and Mailchimp)
- The average person receives 1,216 emails per month, compared to only 178 text messages (Tatango)
- 41% of smartphone users say they would be lost without SMS (Acision)
- 1 person walked into a bear while texting (https://www.youtube.com/watch?v=QCAntD1-DIk)

(Statistics courtesy of http://blog.oxygen8.com/)

4. **Mobile Optimization.** The idea here is to make sure that the website of the business is compatible with and optimized for mobile devices, that is if the business is seeking to get traffic from those mobile devices. However, while it is true that Internet usage is transitioning to mobile, it does not mean that a website is necessarily going to be left in the dust if the owner does not make an effort to look good on a mobile device. For instance, in the old days of mobile phones, those devices were unable to view an HTML website. So for a while, people were saying that every website had to embrace a new format to avoid being left in the dust. Well, today, all the smartphones can view standard webpages for the most part, while other devices like tablet PCs are designed with Internet browsing in mind. Another example would be the iPad, which people like to use because it has a screen big enough to view a website in full size. The marketer's website does not have to be mobile optimized to look good on an iPad. On the one hand, one can still have a successful website even if it is not catering to mobile users. On the other hand, why not cater to them?

Accomplishing this route would be complicated but very feasible. One would be to create a dedicated mobile version of the website. Another would be to use a responsive web design, which allows any site to look good on any screen size. Third would be to simply use a WordPress plug-in or a mobile-ready theme, in which case, this is the easiest route.

Creating a mobile version of a website

This is a good option for someone who is serious about targeting mobile users and making one's website accessible. It is also possible to create multiple versions of the site in different mobile formats so that traditional old-school mobile phone users who are still using the WAP standard will be able to see the site.

First, in order to serve mobile website to mobile users, there is a need to detect and redirect mobile users to the owner's mobile site. In other words, here, there can be two or more versions of website: a website for WAP users, a version for iPhones, a version for iPads, a version for Android phones, and so on. And then there are several ways of detecting and redirecting mobile users, all of which are somewhat technical. Currently, the best way to do it is to detect the user agent with HTAccess, or PHP, ASP, or JavaScript. The script detects what kind of device the visitor is using and if they are using a mobile device, it will automatically send them to the mobile version of the website.

Where now is the mobile version of the website? It can be anywhere although generally, people will put it at something like m.example.com; that's pretty much the industry standard. Or it could be example.com/mobile and simply put it in a directory. It is also possible to register the .mobi extension for the domain, so the website address would be example.mobi. However, that can present some SEO problems, because in that case, there are two domains competing against each other with some of the same content. A better option would be to register the .mobi and simply redirect it to the mobile version of the website on the same domain like m.example.com.

Once everything is set up, here are some tips to keep in mind when designing the mobile version of the site:
- Keep the layout simple.
- Make sure that the website is fast. People on their smartphones are not going to sit there and wait a long time for the site to load.
- Do not use too many images. Smaller images load faster.
- Avoid flash, JavaScript, and other unnecessary scripts.
- Avoid frames.
- Design for thumbs rather than mouse clicks. For instance, put a space between the buttons and make

them large enough so people can click them with their thumbs.
- Prioritize content. Do not just take all the content of the entire site and put it all on the mobile site. Just include the most important stuff.
- Make sure to employ easy navigation; put a home button at the top and bottom of each page along with the back button. Scroll in one direction only, preferably vertical scroll.
- If possible, do not make the mobile site too wide.
- Focus on one action. The same principle applies for all webpages, but even more so for pages of your mobile site. In designing the site, take note of the one thing that people should do when they visit the website. Is it to opt-in? Is it to buy the product? Is it to click on an ad? Whatever that one thing is, focus on that one action.

The easiest way to serve a website to mobile users is to use a WordPress plug-in or a WordPress theme that has mobile compatibility built into it. For those who are starting a new site, the easiest solution may be to simply find a theme that is mobile ready. Go to WordPress.org and click on themes and do a search for mobile. From there, several themes will appear, automatically displaying a mobile version of the site to mobile users. Meanwhile, for those who already have a WordPress theme, use a plug-in instead. Just go to WordPress.org/extend/plugins and look at the many plug-ins that instantly generate the mobile version of the site. Some of those plug-ins include WordPress mobile pack, WordPress mobile edition, WP mobile detector, WP touch, BAAP mobile edition, and OnSwipe, which is specifically for iPad and tablets.

Mobile SEO

Mobile SEO pertains to search results that people would see when they conduct a search from a mobile device. This is something that is constantly fluctuating because the search engines are still trying to figure out the best way to handle this. A good approach to take is simply to combine a traditional SEO approach with mobile best practices. In other words, regardless of which method is used to deliver content to mobile users, the marketer would want to optimize that content using traditional SEO methods.

In mobile search, shorter keywords are usually better. The long tail approach may be a little less effective for mobile search. Google also has a protocol for mobile sitemaps. Keep the layout simple, make sure it is fast, avoid flash, avoid JavaScript and other unnecessary scripts, avoid frames, design for thumbs rather than mouse-clicks, prioritize content, and make sure to employ easy navigation.

Here are other tips that website owners and marketers might find helpful:

1. Check the speed of the page and get some specific optimization tips at pagespeed.googlelabs.com. For instance, the site to check is oracularmarketing.com. Pagespeed will give the user a link of specific suggestions to improve the speed of the site. From there, a mobile report will be generated and this report will provide specific suggestions in optimizing the site for mobile devices.

2. Test the website under various mobile devices at http://mobiletest.me/. This site gives the website owner an idea of what the site actually looks like on various mobile devices, including how fast it loads and which files on the site are slowing it down.

3. Google has provided http://howtogomo.com to teach web designers how to make web properties mobile friendly. There are several notable things one can do here:

Test the website; see what the current site looks like on a mobile phone; and Google will create and give you a free report with personalized recommendation of how to optimize your site for mobile phones.

4. Do a mobile search using google.com/m. Google shows you the results that users will see when they are searching from a mobile device.

There is one more ingredient for mobile traffic that fits in the category of accessibility and compatibility—that is targeting mobile users with context especially acceptable to mobile devices, such as QR codes. QR codes should be used in any offline advertising. They can be placed anywhere from business cards, shirts, stickers, and on countless other items. QR code generators are available on the Internet for free. Marketers and business owners can create one that can be scanned using a smartphone. When scanned, this will take the user to a mobile landing page set up on the marketer's website. Use QR codes with Facebook and Twitter.

The bottom line here is that a huge portion of mobile internet use is devoted to social media, so marketers can attract more of that traffic if they are involved with social media. Use video, for a huge percentage of mobile traffic is devoted to watching videos. Also, consider targeting mobile users with stuff that they're particularly likely to access with their mobile phones, such as coupons, ringtones, travel information, games and puzzles, mobile ebooks, restaurant and business reviews, local business info, and weather.

Summary:

It boils down to this, you need to decide whether mobile marketing should be a priority for your business. If it is not a priority now, at a minimum, take a look at simple ways to make your site mobile friendly. For instance, if your site or blog is built out on Wordpress it is a simple plug-in upload and activation to make your entire site/blog mobile friendly.

If it is a priority (and it should be) then implement every strategy available to make your websites mobile friendly and build a marketing campaign to attract as much mobile traffic as possible.

About the Author

My job is to help you make more money in less time by setting up predictive marketing campaigns for your business, product or service. I have used these systems in my own businesses for 7-years using Traffic Geyser & now teach what I know. I've been certified to consult with you on the use of the TrafficGeyser2.0 Instant Customer & Author Expert Marketing Machines. If you need a jump start on your campaign just reach out.

CERTIFICATIONS & ACCOLADES
- AUTHOR EXPERT MARKETING MACHINES CERTIFIED EXPERT
- TRAFFIC GEYSER 2.0 CERTIFIED EXPERT
- TOP GUN CONSULTING TOOLKIT CERTIFIED EXPERT
- PUBLISH AND PROFIT CERTIFIED EXPERT
- FACEBOOK BUSINESS ACCOUNT RETARGETED AD MANAGEMENT
- GOOGLE ENGAGE FOR AGENCIES AUTHORIZED AGENT
- INSTANT CUSTOMER MASTERY CERTIFIED EXPERT

- ☐ **CALIFORNIA REAL ESTATE BROKER LICENSEE**
- **UNIVERSITY OF WISCONSIN – BA/MASS COMMUNICATIONS/PHOTOGRAPHY**

SERVICES

Call me for a free 20-minute consultation to determine the scope & scale of your project needs. I have a video studio in La Mesa, CA & another in Las Vegas. II have an outsource team in place and we can JV on projects, or I can help you with any aspect of your marketing campaigns in an advisory capacity:

- One-on-one coaching
- SEO & keyword strategy
- Video Marketing
- Livecasting
- Podcasting
- Social Marketing
- PPC Google
- Facebook Display Advertising
-

My company uses all of the tools inside of TrafficGeyser & InstantCustomer & I have trained staff using them every day to promote businesses, products & services.

To learn more about Steve Laurvick and how he helps make his clients use mobile, social and video marketing campaigns to increase return-on-investestment visit www.askame.com or subscribe to his email list and learn all about advanced marketing techniques by texting your name and email to +1 (858) 633-8332.

Social Media—Leveraging Your Brand and Creating Buzz
by Jerry Dreessen, Melodie Rush and Karol Clark

Social media is a great way to promote your business and create more buzz. It doesn't matter if you have a brick-and-mortar business or a completely online business. It also doesn't matter if you sell products or services. Using social media to create more buzz is something all business owners need to do. It's one of the best ways, that's really practically free, to get the word out about your business. Imagine taking an idea, creating an image of it, getting feedback from people, and then having it go "viral" through social media. And all of that marketing is for FREE. Companies spend up to 15% of their gross income on aggressive marketing. Using social media helps level the playing field for a lot of businesses. You would do yourself a huge favor by adding social media into your marketing Swiss Army knife.

When you consider the fact that so many people are on social media (and not just on it; they keep it with them in the form of their mobile devices almost at all times), it becomes clear that you need to use social media to promote your business. At no other time in history has a business been able to be so close to their customers at all times. Imagine being only one second away from your buyers when you announce a new product, or a sale on an existing product. E-commerce has revolutionized how we do business, and more and more companies are building apps as the demand for apps keep rising.

Interact with Your Audience

The more you interact with your audience, the more likely they are to help you create buzz for items that you want to pass the word about. The audience won't feel as if they are being sold if you use social media regularly to interact with your audience. They will be more likely to share what you say if you're there all the time too. I've always enjoyed hearing directly from the owner of the company and reading their posts and answering questions from visitors. It gives you a sense of "knowing them" and helps bridge the gap from a stranger to a customer.

Use Facebook for Events

It's free to use, so you might as well use Facebook events to spread the word about your events on social media. It's a great way to create buzz for an event because people can easily share it. It's also a great way to leverage free publicity on social media. Nothing is better than free to promote something important to your business. It's getting a lot easier using Facebook tools and only pennies a click to promote your post to others. Adding "Share this post to [niche] lovers" will also help engage more people and direct them to your product or service.

Use Google Hangouts On Air

If you have any events or grand message to send, a really good way to get buzz going is to have a Google Hangout On Air. This is a live event that you have some people join, and others watch it as it's happening live. You can do a roundtable event, discussing other important events to come, or sales, or whatever you want to. People will get to view you in action and share it with their friends too. If you want high exposure, make your hangout public to anyone, and put the keywords in your title—example: "Top 10 dog houses—a Review". And then of course the Google Hangout would be you interviewing dog house owners or builders, and would include a link to your product or webpage where the viewer could go to and make a purchase (dog house plans, how to train your dog, doggie treats...).

Tease Your Audience

Send out infographics, images, and more about your new product or service in advance of it being live. As you create parts of your product, share it. A book cover, a few paragraphs from your new book, and some graphics and images that pique the interest of your audience will go far to create buzz and excitement about your new product or service. You can also drop in a "survey monkey" link with the page, asking the audience what they would like to see/change/have or what they like/don't like about your product, which will begin to build a list of people who are ready to buy your next product.

Blog and Share

Most people don't think of blogging as social media, but the moment you open your comments up, it is social. So blog about what's going on in your business and in your life if it fits, and open up those blogs to commenting. Ask for comments to get it started and respond to the comments to keep the discussion going. Using keywords for your title as well as in your content will help the "google bots" index your post—sometimes reaching page one of Google for some people.

Creating buzz about your business using social media is a quick way to get people talking about your business. It's as simple as setting up an account and getting started using the content you already have. Don't delay.

The top social media markets:

- Google +
- LinkedIn
- Pinterest
- Instagram
- Snapchat
- Facebook
- Vine
- Twitter
- Tumblr
- Yelp
- Blogs (Blogger, Wordpress)
- YouTube

Which social networking site should you use?

You are probably asking the question "Which social networking site should I use?" It all depends on your clients or customers and what you are trying to accomplish. Each one has its strengths and weaknesses in connecting with certain demographics and for certain purposes.

Google+ (http://www.googlepluss.com) is good for specific subjects or interests. Over the last couple years it has grown in popularity. It also has special power since it is connected to Google Hangouts on air and has a special relations ship with the largest search engine Google. Google+'s largest audience is 18-34 year olds.

YouTube (http://www.youtube.com) is an online Video hosting service. Many people do not think of it as a social networking site, but with the ability to share videos and comment on those videos makes it very powerful for building your brand and sharing your knowledge. It is also great for SEO with the Google connection.

LinkedIn (http://www.linkedin.com) is often thought of as the resume site, but it is much more than that. It is known as the corporate, professional or employee site for social media. It is great for coaching, consulting, copywriting, web development, business development, partnerships and recruitment. Keep posts here on the professional level. This is not the place for cute cat videos. It is a great place to connect with clients, if you clients are in a business or professional role. The average income for a Linkedin user is considerably higher than for the other social media channels.

Pinterest (http://www.pinterest.com) is all about images, especially photos and infographics. Pinterest is all about creating images or videos for your business or service that people will want to share. The users of Pinterest tend to be a high percentage of women with higher than average incomes. The Pinterest user also spends the most amount of money of any of the social media channels.

Instagram (http://www.instagram.com) is also an image sharing platform, mostly pictures, although videos can also be shared. It is most useful if you are in a business that is visually focused. Great for business like food, products, fashion, travel, etc. Almost one quarter of the users are teens.

Snapchat (http://www.snapchat.com) is a photo sharing direct messaging app primarily used by 13-25 year olds. It is unique because images and messages are only available for a short amount of time. Snapchat is great for product and brand awareness for Gen Z. Some companies are using it to deliver time sensitive offers such as coupons or giveaways. Roughly 70% of the users are women.

Facebook (http://www.facebook.com) is by far the largest social site with over 1.5 billion users. Facebook is for building relationships and for socializing. Keep your posts here entertaining. People use Facebook to connect with others. Be sure that your information post vs. selling posts are 6 to 1. Facebook is great for customer engagement and brand exposure. There are slightly more males to females and the largest age group 35-54. Facebook is also attractive to the people over 65 who are online.

Vine (https://vine.co/)is a short 6-second videos service. Made popular initially by Twitter. It is mostly used by companies for showcasing new products or services. The primary user is 18-21 year olds and weekends are most popular time.

Twitter (http://www.twitter.com)is great for instant news and short conversations. Tweets have a short life! So you want to repeat tweets to be most effective. Twitter is great for customer engagement, traffic to your website and brand recognition. The users are 65% female and typically ages from 25-54.

Tumblr (https://www.tumblr.com) works well for companies that have a good strong content. You can share text, photos, links and videos. Men have more followers on Tumblr but women have more repins.

Yelp (http://www.yelp.com) is for a brick and mortar business like restaurants, dentists, or car repair. It is great to help local businesses be found through smart phone app or through online searches.

Wordpress and **Blogger** (http://www.blogger.com) are the 2 most common blogging sites. Wordpress has both a free hosted (http://www.workpress.org) and self-hosted (http://www.workpress.com) services and is the largest of the blogging platforms. Blogger is a free web blogging tool from Google, which works well for getting SEO rankings with Google. Many people have had success using Blogger to sell affiliate products and services.

Blogs in general are very popular form of content sharing. Almost 25% of Internet time is spent on blogs and social networks. Companies with blogs have way more inbound links than those without and blogs generate tons of leads for B2B marketers.

For more Internet facts and statistics check out the following links:
- ☐ http://www.mediabistro.com/alltwitter/social-media-statistics-2014_b57746
- ● http://www.searchenginejournal.com/growth-social-media-2-0-infographic/77055/

You may be asking yourself the question do I need to use all of these social media channels? Probably not! If you or your business are new to social media then start with the one that is most likely to have your intended audience. You can add others as time permits. You will pretty quickly see which ones allow you to interact with your clients or potential clients.

Each of these services are free to join and set up. A smart, savvy business person would be wise to open up an account for each of these with their business "keywords" and begin writing little "blurbs" about what they do at least once a week, each time pointing a link to their website or product. They could even write out 52 different blurbs all at once and have a whole year's marketing done, and then add occasional or topical comments as events happen.

There are also some great services such as HootSuite (www.hootsuite.com) or IFTT (www.iftt.com) that will take a single one-time post and distribute it all across your social network—a true time saver/savior!

There's No Buzz until You Put Your Social Media Plan into Action

It is easy to feel overwhelmed when it comes to all of the social media options available. However, with a firm grasp of your audience (your ideal client or Avatar), helpful (often conversational) content relevant to the information they seek (including a clear call to action as appropriate) and a plan for timely delivery, you have a recipe for social media success.

You can do this in 4 steps:

1. Sign up for your free social media accounts and customize them to your brand. As mentioned earlier, you want to create your accounts with your business keywords in mind. If you are unsure, you can confirm what these keywords are through a free Google Keyword Planner search. Look at your strategic plan – what are you trying to build? What is your ultimate goal? Are you promoting a larger corporation or focused on a specific product/service? Are you building your personal brand? If so, you could also build it around your name (although this can be limiting down the road).

You do not have to participate in every single form of social media out there. You should research which option is most likely to have your ideal client (as outlined earlier in this chapter). Realize that this is usually more than one option but focus your energy where you will be most likely to reach your target audience so you get a positive return on your investment of time, creativity and effort. If that is too overwhelming, start with one and build from there as you are ready. The important thing is to begin!

2. If possible, find someone trustworthy to take responsibility for managing your social media. This doesn't mean that they also have to create the content but having one person who consistently posts according to your editorial calendar is helpful. If you are "it", then make sure you set aside time so your messages are posted consistently. As mentioned earlier, you can schedule your posts ahead of time in many social media forums which make your time management much easier. Do not make this harder than it has to be. Start out simple and expand if and when it is appropriate. There are also tools that will take on video or article and send it to multiple media sources - your own 'syndication' so to speak (i.e. Traffic Geyser). You likely have content already created that can be utilized. It doesn't have to be long (often the shorter the better). You can also use your content in a variety of ways as described in the case study below. Let's face it, some people like video, some like audio and some like to digest information via a written article. You can appeal to the masses with such multicasting.

3. Take time to create a simple editorial calendar for at least one week in advance or preferably longer. Once again, keep it as simple as possible and manageable for your particular business/situation. Similar to how we all find various ways to manage our daily/weekly/monthly calendars for optimal productivity; editorial calendars need to be customized to what works for you. Some sample ideas are included in the case study below.

4. Implement!!! Planning is great but unless you implement your plan, you will not be able to leverage your

brand and create your 'buzz' that will bring you new customers and nurture the ones you already have (one of your biggest assets). Use many (legal) images – people respond very well to images and videos. Something eye-catching and out of the ordinary. Also, don't forget to share and ask others to share because usually, they will!

Never before has marketing been so easy and affordable. Social media is fresh, fun and an easy way to get the word out about you and your business. Explore various options and then focus on the ones that work the best for you. It's "noisy" out there. Use your creativity (or hire someone creative and experienced) so you stand out in your niche!

Case Study – Center for Weight Loss Success, Newport News, VA www.cfwls.com:

The Center for Weight Loss Success is a successful comprehensive entity that provides weight loss services including weight loss surgery, medical weight loss, fitness and nutritional products under the direction of double board certified surgeon – Dr. Thomas W. Clark. The center attracts clients from in and around the United States. Services are provided in a concierge style focused on optimal customer service and satisfaction.

The Center for Weight Loss Success caters to motivated people who are interested in losing 5 pounds to hundreds of pounds. They offer exclusive on-site and online weight loss programs such as Weight Management University™, a comprehensive 12 month post weight loss surgery program called Weight Management University for Weight Loss Surgery™ and My Weight Loss Academy™ as well as quick jump start programs. In addition, Dr. Clark is arguably one of the most experienced bariatric surgeons in the US having performed over 4,000 weight loss procedures since 1994. He and his staff are passionate about helping people not only lose weight but understand how to keep it off for life.

Business situation

The arena of bariatric surgery has become extremely competitive. In addition, most surgeons are now owned by hospital systems in lieu of navigating the unstable environment and uncertainties that comes with having an independent practice. This makes marketing extremely difficult since health system competitors have much deeper marketing pockets and can utilize additional higher expense marketing avenues such as radio and TV.

Dr. Clark and his team have remained independent by design. They want to be able to control their destiny and cater to the motivated weight loss client who desires comprehensive services and customer service that outshines the competition. Their niche is not only clients with insurance but those who have weight loss excluded on their policies and are interested in a high quality, affordable cash pay alternative for surgical and non-surgical weight loss with outstanding customer service, education and follow-up.

These situations, along with the addition of a retail store and fitness center in 2011, resulted in the need for an outstanding online presence and social media marketing plan that includes quality education.

Social Media Plan of Action

Following the 4 step process above, the following plan was developed:

1. Social media accounts were set up. With weight loss, creativity was necessary since many obvious choices were

taken. Accounts were set up and customized. You can see the URL's below:

- **Facebook** (www.facebook.com/weightlossdrclark)
- **Twitter** (www.twitter.com/docweightloss)
- **Pinterest** (www.pinterest.com/cfwlsva/)
- **YouTube** (www.youtube.com/docweightloss)
- **Blog** (www.cfwls.com/blog)
- **LinkedIn** (www.linkedin.com/company/dr-clark's-center-for-weight-loss-success)
- **Google+**(https://plus.google.com/+CenterForWeightLossSuccessNewportNews/posts)
- **Tumblr** – (http://cfwls.tumblr.com/)

As third party software evolves, there have been many opportunities to make one post and have it automatically delivered to the various platforms. Use this if it works for you. For video, YouTube has a convenient option to share your content directly from your post to nearly all social media options.

2. A motto to live by is to "surround yourself with the highest quality people possible". This relates to those with a good value system, integrity, work ethic and complementary habits. Once you have your awesome team in place, treat them well! The Center for Weight Loss Success has a dynamic team that makes weight loss fun!

The staff that has an interest and talent for social media and e-mail marketing integrated these duties into their routine. This primarily includes the Education & Fitness Coordinator, Retail Sales Manager and Practice Administrator. Fortunately, Dr. Clark is king of content and great on camera along with several talented personal trainers. He researches constantly and helps to keep the staff and his patients armed with the latest information to help them achieve their goals. He runs his own webinars each week along with 2 popular podcasts each week. All of the staff do their part and are ready with their cameras when something fun or exciting is happening (like when someone is on the scale and hits their 100 pound weight loss mark). Of course, having wonderful patients who are willing to share their stories helps too.

3. Everyone contributes to the editorial calendar and it is created/managed by the Education & Fitness Coordinator. Prior to the next year, the leadership team selects a theme and monthly newsletter topics. The editorial calendar then carries out the newsletter monthly themes along with responding to any weight loss topics "in the news". Face-to-face outreach is also important by Dr. Clark and the Administrator (his wife) and they actually now consult for other practices through Weight Loss Practice Builder (www.WeightLossPracticeBuilder.com) so they can help others integrate successful turn-key programs as well. Obesity is an epidemic and America needs programs that result in optimal long-term success! The more healthcare practitioners with access to these successful programs, the better. Better yet, it is a way for them to help their patients see results, generate extra revenue and increase their referral base.

From the calendar, we create a specific editorial calendar that specifies topics for social media posts, who is doing the post, keywords, events, book launches and weekly e-mails. A sample is included below:

Social Media & Marketing Campaign
for cfwls.com

February						Focus: Rx for Loving Yourself
						Events: Nutrition Store event 2/17/14, Support Group 2/19/14

	January 27th - February 2nd					Newsletter Headline: Rx for Loving Yourself
	Monday	Tuesday	Wednesday	Thursday	Friday	Articles: Increasing your libido, self-esteem, love your body
Social Media Posts: Dawn	Fitness	Testimonials	Podcasts	Inspiration	Recipe	Keywords: libido, self-esteem, hormones, estrogen, testosterone,
Twitter:	Dr. Clark	Dr. Clark	Dr. Clark	Dr. Clark	Dr. Clark	LWUSA Newsletter: Weight Loss or Water Loss?/Hummus Crusted Chicken
E-Mail (LWUSA & Newsletter):	Dawn	Dawn				LWUSA Webinar: Ideas to Use RIGHT NOW to Lose Weight
You Tube Video Post & Link to FB:				Dawn		DocWeightLossPodcast: Hormone Havoc
Pinterest:	Fitness	Testimonials	Podcasts	Inspiration	Recipe	WeightLossSurgerySuccess Podcast: Iodine and Your Thyroid Health
Blog Posts:	Education				Recipe	Fitness Specials: Begin advertising 8 week challenge - ROCK those JEANS!
						Store Specials: Weight Loss Vitamins
WMU Lifestyle Topic: Lifestyle Changes						Infusionsoft Campaign: Weight Loss Vitamin Package
WMU Fitness Focus: Resistance Tubing						PCP Activities:
						B2B Activities:
Retail Emailer	Cat K		Cat K			Print Ad: Health Journal
						Events: Cardio Fitness Challenge
						National Health Observances: Heart Month
						Ideas:

	February 3rd - February 9th					Newsletter Headline: Rx for Loving Yourself
	Monday	Tuesday	Wednesday	Thursday	Friday	Articles: Increasing your libido, self-esteem, love your body
Social Media Posts: Dawn	Fitness	Testimonials	Podcasts	Inspiration	Recipe	Keywords: libido, self-esteem, hormones, estrogen, testosterone,
Twitter:	Dr. Clark	Dr. Clark	Dr. Clark	Dr. Clark	Dr. Clark	LHR Newsletter: Tips to Surviving the Weekend Without Weight Gain/Protein Waffles
E-Mail (LWUSA & Newsletter):	Dawn	Dawn				LHR Webinar: Which Vitamins are Vital for Weight Loss?
You Tube Video Post & Link to FB:				Dawn		DocWeightLossPodcast:
Pinterest:	Fitness	Testimonials	Podcasts	Inspiration	Recipe	WeightLossSurgerySuccess Podcast: The Importance of Core Exercise
Blog Posts:	Education				Recipe	Fitness Specials: Sign-ups for 8 week challenge - ROCK those JEANS!
						Store Specials:
WMU Lifestyle Topic: Staying Healthy						Infusionsoft Campaign:
WMU Fitness Focus: Walking						PCP Activities:
						B2B Activities:
Retail Emailer	Cat K		Cat K			Print Ad: Health Journal
						Events: Store Event 2/4

4. The plan is in place. Now execute and discuss the plan of action once a week in the event changes are necessary, some newsworthy story needs to be addressed, a new best-selling book is launched or a new product/service is offered.

Your plan can be something similar, something more complex, or something as simple as an engaging post 2-3 times per week. Stay focused on your ideal client and what they really want and need (which is not necessarily always the same thing). Post with integrity, use only approved photos and stay true to your mission.

About the Authors

Jerry Dreessen has been in online marketing for over 10 years. He has read and studied multiple gurus on the subject of website construction, design, and Search Engine Optimization (SEO). He has implemented what he has studied to boost his online presence in his local market as a Chiropractor (videos, ebooks, landing pages), and founded his own company to provide website services as well. He is an Instant Customer Certified Consultant and has helped many people launch their business with the Done With You service. When he is not treating patients, designing websites, teaching or learning, he likes to hike and camp in the Pacific Northwest forests, and sail Hobie cats with his wife and 3 kids.

Melodie Rush is a trained Statistician and holds a technical MBA. She has presented and consulted with many Fortune 500 companies, both domestically and internationally. Being a geek has not always been cool, but it has certainly given her the opportunity to teach and consult on many analytical topics across many industries. Her biggest strength is relating technical information to non-technical folks. She has an uncanny ability to simplify topics and chunk them into small bite-size pieces that even those afraid of technology can understand. Melodie is an experienced speaker both in person and via virtual webinars, having led more than 2000 presentations since 1996. She knows what works and what doesn't when it comes to doing presentations. She is the author of the soon-to-be-released book *Webinar Strategies*. Melodie launched We Create MVPs to share her knowledge and expertise by helping those new to doing presentations (either live or webinars) become powerful, influential presenters. Additionally, Melodie works with her clients to become recognized experts in their chosen niche through video, social media and online marketing. She most recently became an Instant Customer/Traffic Geyser coach and is a certified professional with Author Expert Marketing Machines. Her experience includes creating and implementing campaigns, surveys, analyzing data, and coordinating presentations, from 1 hour to 2 days. Melodie lives in Colorado with her husband and two cats. She loves to travel, scrapbook, and play with technology. In her spare time, she volunteers at the Denver Zoo as a Docent.

To download my 2 free bonuses:

1. "Establishing your Outcome Blueprint", a one-page worksheet to help you identify the outcome for your presentation

2. "The 10 Biggest Mistakes to Avoid when Creating Slides". This guide will help you avoid the most common mistakes people make when creating and utilizing slides in their presentations.

Visit www.melodierush.com/ShareYourExpertise or text your name and email address to 720-897-1999 or scan this QR Code

Karol Clark is formally trained as master's prepared Registered Nurse in the field of women's health, medical and surgical weight loss, and nutrition. Karol is also a marketing expert with over 20 years of experience as a hospital administrator, surgical practice administrator, and consultant. Karol has helped her husband, Dr. Thomas W. Clark, create and launch four Amazon best-selling books. She has also helped him integrate successful non-traditional medical marketing strategies such as podcasting, product development, webinars, and membership sites into his busy bariatric surgery practice. Karol utilizes these skills to help other professionals attract the clients they want, become best-selling authors, and grow their practice while enjoying the journey along the way. Karol is also the founder and CEO of *Weight Loss Practice Builder* where she, her husband and her team assist physicians, healthcare practitioners, and fitness professionals to integrate a profitable turnkey weight loss program into their practice. Karol is a certified professional with Author Expert Marketing Machines and Make Market Launch. She lives in Virginia with her husband and their four children. You can reach Karol via LinkedIn or through any of her business sites:

www.CFWLS.com
www.WeightLossPracticeBuilder.com
www.YourBestSellerBook.com
www.CenterforHormoneHealthandWellness.com

Trade Shows
by Sandi Masori

Trade shows are a great way to get your message or brand out there.

Before you even begin, though, you need to figure out what is your objective? That is, what are you hoping to get out of the trade show?

Are you looking to build a list?

Are you trying to increase your branding and name recognition?

Are you trying to make sales or take orders on the spot?

In this chapter, we are going to focus on trade shows, where the objective is list building. For purposes of simplicity, we're going to pretend that you either have a table-top in an expo, or a 10x10 to 20x20 booth.

There are several things we need to talk about:

- Booth Design

- The Offer

- The Attraction

Let's start with booth design: It doesn't really matter if you have a booth that's been designed by an expensive prop company or just a table, some balloons, and some banners. The main idea is that your booth should attract attention and feel welcoming.

Don't put the table across the front of the booth and sit behind it. Put the table either in the back of the booth or to the side. The subtle message is "come on in and hang out".

The colors should be interesting and in line with your corporate image and values.

17 Secrets from a Marketing Mastermind

Balloons are a great way to attract attention to a booth and also to make people feel comfortable. They also can get those opt-in signs right up at eye-level.

Let's talk about balloons for a moment. While balloons shouldn't be considered "cheap", they can be very budget friendly for the amount of impact they provide. Also, the unions often don't care if the balloon people bring in their own equipment and set up. This can save you a lot of money in drayage.

For a simple eye-catching display, I recommend two air-filled framed columns for a booth, or an air-filled table-top arch for venues where you only get a table and not a full booth. The main idea behind either style is that they can put the opt-in signs up at eye-level where people can see them and take the appropriate action.

I recommend printing your call to action as an 11 x 17 (portrait orientation) laminated and mounted sign.

So, now that we've talked about what it might look like, let's talk about what's on those signs, or in other words, the offer.

This is probably the most important part of it all. In my experience, contests do best for trade shows. The prize or giveaway is critical. A lot of people want to give away an iPad. On the one hand, it's a pretty juicy prize and many people will enter to win it. The problem with giving away an iPad is that the only thing that that tells you about the people who opted-in is that they like gadgets. It says nothing as to whether they're interested in your product or service. If you sell gadgets, that may be perfect. If, on the other hand, you are a chiropractor, that doesn't tell you anything at all about how they feel about functional and alternative medicine.

So, this is the hardest part of the whole thing; what can you give away that will be congruent with the products or services that you offer, but, at the same time, not devalue those same services? It's tricky to figure this one out, and I suggest that you spend some time thinking about it.

Here are the criteria that the prize must meet: It must be sufficiently juicy or interesting that people would want it, but also connected to your products or services so that people opting in would indicate an interest in what you do. For example, one client of mine had great success giving away a photo glossary of what words to use when placing an order for special event decorations. Another client of mine had success letting people enter to win a year's subscription to their website (a membership site), while also giving a two-week trial membership to everyone who entered. Still another client, a chiropractor, had success giving away a video series of simple back exercises. As I own a balloon company, I have had great success with a contest for a limited balloon setup.

You may get fewer total leads, but the leads that you do get will be much better qualified, and, at the end of the day, do you want a big giant list of random people, or do you want more customers? The more targeted your list, the less time you'll waste on following up with people who are not interested in you.

Now that we've talked about the offer, let's talk about how people opt-in.

I've had the best success using a digital opt-in system where prospects can place themselves on your list by texting their name and email to a unique phone number that drops them right into your list and initiates the auto-responder sequence. (That means that it puts them on your mailing list and begins sending them a series of pre-written e-mails.)

Using this system, you can also ask some follow-up qualifying questions via text message. This is also automated.

For prospects who "don't do texting", they can call the same unique phone number and leave a voicemail with their name and email. This will trigger the auto-responder sequence as well.

What would this look like? Well check it out:

Here's an example (follow the directions in bold to see live example): -
Text your
NAME and EMAIL
to 858 207 4855

Pretty cool, huh? Here's an example of the type of sign you might use:

17 Secrets from a Marketing Mastermind

Now let's talk more about getting people into the booth and the jobs of the booth staff.

I'm often asked about hiring "booth babes" or models to draw people over. This is something that you want to be careful with. If you're selling something that caters to a predominantly male audience, then this may work. But if you want to appeal to women as well, beware of using scantily clad models; they can be a turn-off.

Far more important than how they look is how is their energy? What is their attitude? You want to hire "barkers" who are very friendly and energetic. I can't stress enough how important this is—if your booth staff is not energetic and excessively outgoing, you will not do nearly as well as you could.

You want someone with the personality of a cheerleader, someone who will "grab" people as they walk by, give them a huge smile, and get that prospect to pull out their phone and opt-in to your list.

That barker doesn't need to know *anything* about your business; in fact, it's better if they don't. Why, you may ask? Because the barkers most important and only job is to get people to opt-in to the list. If they are getting into detailed conversations with people, they will miss the opportunity to stop more people and get them to opt-in.

Inside the booth there should be another person who is the expert or salesperson who is responsible for answering questions. This expert should only spend time with the warmer prospects—those who are asking questions and wanting to learn more about the company, product, or service. All questions and inquiries should be directed to the designated expert or salesperson.

The front person, or the barker as we've been calling them, is the first person that is seen, and they greet and grab prospective prospects. The expert/ salesperson answers questions and gives more information.

Now let's talk about some of the fatal mistake that so many booths make... not engaging!

I can't tell you how often I go to trade shows and am going past the booths and see the booth attendants either reading, playing with their phone, or having a deep conversation with each other. When that happens, it sends the message that you don't have time or interest in talking to the prospects.

Everyone in your booth needs to be alert, friendly, and open. No reading, sitting behind the table, or playing on the phone.

Discourage your people from clustering together and talking to each other, as this can send a very unwelcoming signal to your prospects. This seems so obvious, but the next time you're at a trade show, walk up and down the aisles and see how many booths you see violating this very simple rule. You will be shocked!

Let's go back to the opt-in itself. Using a text-based system, the process might look like this:

A prospect walks past the booth.

Booth Attendant (BA) with big smile: Hi! How are you? Have you already entered to win the year's supply of blue widgets give-away? It's a $5,000 value!

Prospect (P): No, I haven't. I'd love to get free blue widgets. What do I need to do?

BA: Oh, it's super simple, take out your phone and I'll help you. Just text your name and email to 555-555-5555, or scan the QR code and follow the directions. Please make sure that you put both your name and email in the same message.

Once you do that, you'll receive a couple of follow-up questions so that we can learn more about the ways that you use blue widgets. You must answer those questions in order to be eligible to win.

P: Are you going to sell my info?

BA: Of course not; this is only used for our own marketing purposes. We promise not to spam you, and you can unsubscribe at any time.

P: Sound ok, I guess I'll try. How do I know if I've won?

BA: We'll send out an email on Monday announcing the winner. Be sure to keep an eye on your inbox for it.

P: Cool, thanks. By the way, I was wondering, do you only sell blue widgets? I'm looking for red?

BA: That's a great question. Let me introduce you to Bob, he's an expert on all things widget and can answer all of your questions.

P: Perfect, thanks!

Let's talk about the deliverable. You want to send all gifts via email. The reason for this is that you want to train people to go to their email and pull you out of junk mail when they're most motivated. And that's when they're waiting for the cool prize that you offered.

The awesome thing about using an automated system like this is that the email carrying the deliverable (and contact information and the like) is sent to them before they've even walked away from you. You don't have to take a list home and enter people into it; the system will send out the email for whenever you schedule it. And for the prospects, the awesome thing is that they don't have to carry around yet another brochure or booklet that they're probably just going to leave in their hotel room anyway.

So to recap:

- Come up with a compelling give-away that is congruent with your product or service
- Put the compelling give-away behind a digital opt-in and auto-responder system so people can text themselves in for the prize
- Use balloons to create an energetic and inviting booth that stands out from the others around you. (e-mail me if you need help finding someone in any market, Sandi@MarketWithBalloons.com)
- Get excessively energetic booth attendees to act as barkers to stop traffic and help them join the list

- Have a salesperson or expert available in the booth to answer more detailed questions
- Don't make the tragic trade show mistake of being inattentive
- Set auto-responder system to send out initial email as soon as they have subscribed, so that you have followed up with them before they even leave the building.
- Market to all the qualified leads and make more money.

About the Author

Sandi Masori, CBA CMT, is a two-time best-selling author, TV personality, coach, marketer, and balloon expert (and a mom, daughter, and wife). She began her journey into online marketing in 2008 when she wanted to upgrade the Balloon Utopia website and improve her position online.

Masori initially took a "marketing boot camp" class from a fellow balloon artist, and then went on to learn from the teachers he mentioned throughout the course. She found the nuances of the marketing ecosystem fascinating and continued taking higher level courses on the subject. Along the way, she found herself helping others with their marketing and in 2010, she took her first of many certification courses to become a marketing technologist and coach.

Masori began coaching other business owners on how to take control of their own marketing through her WebCoach4You site. She also realized, while working with her corporate clients on the balloon business that she was often being asked to help with some aspect of the event marketing. A light bulb went off and she began to incorporate both balloons and marketing into her corporate business. Market With Balloons (Http://www.MarketWithBalloons.com) was born. She authored and published the best-selling books *The Ultimate Guide To Inflating Your Tradeshow Profits.... With Balloons* and *The Event Planner's Essential Guide To Balloons.*

She has produced hundreds of marketing videos, for both her own channel and those of her clients. At the time of this writing, Sandi's YouTube channel, *Sandi Masori Balloons* (http://www.youtube.com/sandiballoon) has over 7,000 subscribers and 1.7 million views. She has appeared on local and national TV shows like *Daytime* and *The Today Show*. She was quoted as saying, "Everything I learn I try to apply to my own business first, and if it works, then I can I teach it, or do it for others."

Speak To Sell—How To Get People To Buy What You're Selling, Even If They Have No Idea They Want It Or Need It
by Rob Cuesta

A note to readers: this chapter is written by Rob Cuesta, a Brit living in Canada, so you'll need to excuse him if he "incentivises" clients to join his "programmes", etc. It's hard to teach an old dog new tricks, and even harder to teach a Brit to write American ☺

I looked out of the window at the waters of the River Thames flowing lazily past the restaurant, and wondered how to answer the question.

James, my companion at lunch that day had just asked if I'd ever sold from the stage. Technically, the answer was yes. As a manager in one of the world's largest consulting firms, I had often pitched—and won—multi-million dollar consulting projects.

But that wasn't really what he was asking. What James meant was had I sold my own services from the stage at a sales event? That was a very different matter.

In the eight years I had been in business I had avoided making public sales presentations. So I should have answered "no".

Instead I heard myself say, "yes, of course I have!"

And so I set out on a journey that took me from making no sales from the stage to closing over $400,000 in 3 months.

From zero sales per head to walking into a room of 100 people on a Saturday morning *knowing* I will walk out with $100k in sales on Sunday.

From muddling my way through, making every mistake a rookie stage seller makes, to stepping onto the stage knowing exactly how the next hour, day or weekend is going to go.

And in this chapter I'm going to share with you the nine killer mistakes I made—and which I see rookie sellers making all the time—that are pushing your sales through the floor.

If you address these nine points you will transform yourself into a sales rock star, even if you've never closed a single sale from the stage.

Over the last four years I have taught and coached more than 720 people to create and deliver pitches for anything from $200 products to $30,000 or more training programmes and multi-million dollar consulting projects. I have worked with directors of global corporations and with owners of small local businesses.

I am not saying that you will make $100, $10,000 or $100,000 using these techniques—for all I know you'll read this chapter and never apply a single thing in it. All I will say is that when I launched a new business back in 2010 the first thing I did was set up a sales event to get clients.

Solving these nine mistakes is at the heart of the Speak-To-Sell Blueprint I teach my clients in workshops and power days.

So use the nine points as a checklist: it will help you to structure your sales presentations better than ever before, make your offer irresistible, and lead your audience to the close like a pied piper.

Mistake #1. Not Controlling Your State

We all know the stats. People would rather die than have to give a presentation. Giving a presentation ranks higher than snakes and fire on people's list of fears. Yadda, yadda, yadda.

You've also probably been told that a little stage fright is good for you, it gives your performance edge, it shows you care about your audience.

Rubbish.

The moment you walk on stage *to sell* you <u>have</u> to be in control. I don't care if your hand shakes when you give a speech at your best friend's wedding. But I do care if you are anything but composed and in control while you're asking people to give you money.

Look at it from the buyer's point of view.

The guy on stage says he has exactly what you need and it's $5,000. However, he's sweating and his hand is shaking.

Be honest. Do you

a) Think "poor guy, he obviously hates presenting, but the product sounds great. I'll order right away!" and run to the back of the room?
b) Think "hmm, something isn't quite right. It could be nerves about the presentation, but what if it's doubts about what he's saying. I think I'll pass"

I thought so. And that's what your audience would think too.

So you need to control your own state. When I started selling from the stage I had a distinct advantage. As a board-certified trainer of NLP I had a whole range of tools at my disposal to manage my state, which now I share with my clients.

BONUS
If you'd like a simple exercise to do to get you ready to go on stage, visit <u>http://0s4.com/r/TMITB1</u>

Mistake #2. Not Connecting

Have you ever gone food shopping straight after lunch? It's awful. You wander from aisle to aisle, and even though the place is filled with enough food to feed a small African village for a year it's like there's nothing there. Why? Because you're not hungry. And when you're not hungry it doesn't matter what food I put in front of you: you're not going to want it.

I've watched speaker after speaker walk out on stage and bomb because they were talking to an audience that was metaphorically 'stuffed'.

When you start to speak they aren't thinking about their problem. If it's your event and they've just arrived then they're probably thinking about the journey, or the ridiculous price they just paid for a coffee next door, or they're chatting to the person next to them—it can be almost anything, except what you actually want them to be thinking about, which is how bad their problem is and how much they want sit solved.

Your first task, therefore—it's the first step in the Speak-To-Sell Blueprint—is to give them "CPR": **connect** them to their problem, **remind** them of their pain, and get a physical **response**.

So let me ask you a question. Have you ever felt frustrated by how long clients take to buy high-ticket products and services? Have you ever watched a TV shopping channel and wondered how they manage to make it seem so easy, even when they're selling stuff you can't imagine *anyone* wanting? And have you ever been asked to make a presentation and felt fear or stress because you didn't know exactly what to say?

If you answered yes to those questions then congratulations, you're reading the right chapter.

And I just gave you the CP part of CPR. In a real-life presentation I'd have got you to raise your hand—the R.

Mistake #3. Not Getting Permission

Have you ever had someone walk up and try to sell you something when you weren't expecting it? It's bad enough when a sales person in a shop comes up and asks if you want help. Imagine if they walked up and started trying to take an order!

And yet I see so many speakers do the equivalent of this on stage.

Don't assume that, just because someone has sat and listened to you for 50 minutes, you have their permission to sell them something.

One of the key principles I teach my clients is "no surprises". That means you need to get permission right at the start of the talk for the sale later.

Of course you're not going to say "is it OK if I sell to you?" What you *are* going to say is something like "we don't have much time together today, and there's a lot more that I'd like to share with you. *Is it OK if I tell you later how we can continue this journey together and get you to where you need to be?*" You're talking about sharing information later, so the answer is going to be yes. The fact that the information is "you need to sign up for my $2,000 workshop" is irrelevant!

But the **sale** isn't the only thing you need permission for.

You need permission for **being on stage**. You're a stranger. An unknown quantity. For all the audience knows, you are about to waste an hour, a day or even a weekend of their life. So get their permission to talk to them about your topic.

You need to get permission for your **style**. Personally I like to be funny and entertaining when I speak. Some people—indeed some entire audiences—expect me to be very serious, since I'm usually talking about business and money, so I always get the audience to agree that it's OK to be lighthearted. Or maybe you think you're boring but they absolutely have to hear what you have to say. Great. Tell them that and ask if it's OK to be boring because they're going to get immense value out of the talk—they will give you permission.

Whatever your style, get them to say it's OK up front. It will boost your sales later.

Asking permission up front for what you're going to do gives the audience certainty. When something happens they're thinking 'ah yes, this is what I was expecting'. And if there is one thing that is going to help your sales, it's having your audience in a state of certainty!

Mistake #4. Not Telling Your Story

Storytelling is one of the fundamentals of human existence. We were brought up listening to stories. Our ancestors gathered round campfires to share stories. Millions of cinema tickets are sold each year to people who want a good story.

And believe it or not, however humble you may feel, however uninspiring your story may seem to you, however well you may think your audience knows your story, they want to hear it.

They want to know how you know what you know. They want to know about the challenges you faced, and how you overcame them. It's what I call your Expert Journey. And it's a critical part of your sale.

Your story establishes your credibility. Telling your story is the one time when you can—indeed you are encouraged to—brag about your achievements.

Think back to the beginning of this chapter. If I had just said "you should read this chapter because I have taught 720 people how to sell from the stage and I have sold hundreds of thousands of dollars worth of products and services from the stage" your immediate thought would probably have been a four-letter word that rhymes with 'fool'. Instead, because they're part of my story, it was OK to share those achievements with you.

There were also probably parts of my story that you were able to relate to from your own experience, and that created connection between us.

Here's another part of my story. I know how important your story is because a couple of times—once when I was presenting to an audience who already knew my background very well, and once when I presented at the end of a very long day and my slot had been delayed so long that I started my talk an hour after the whole event was supposed to finish (!)—I have been tempted to skip my story. Both times I bombed. I walked out of there with my tail between my legs and zero sales.

That's how important telling your story is.

Mistake #5. Not Having A System

As I said before, your audience wants certainty. They want to know that you know what you're doing; that you've done what you're proposing before.

Certainty sells.

When people buy a McDonalds franchise, they're buying a system: a tried-and-tested system for running a fast food restaurant profitably. It would be cheaper to buy an empty shop, stick your name over the door and do your own thing, but that is a much less certain option.

The same applies in your own business. Your prospects want to know that you have a system to take them from their current state (unhappy and with a problem) to their desired state (happy and free of the problem).

It can be anything from 'the 5 step formula for X' to a whole blueprint for solving the problem, but there has to be a system.

Having your own system also positions you as the expert. Steven Covey was the expert on "The 7 Habits" because he created it. Robert Kiyosaki is the expert on "The Cashflow Quadrant" because he created it. I am the expert on the Speak-To-Sell Blueprint and The Expert Journey because I created them.

You can get started right now creating your system. Think about the result you want to sell: can you break it down into 5-7 steps or key points? That's your system. It needs polishing and perfecting, but you've got the basics. Congratulations!

Mistake #6. Giving Away Too Much/Too Little

Mistake number 6 is one of the two most serious mistakes new (and even experienced) presenters make selling from the stage.

If you're a natural teacher it's hard to hold back. You want your audience to have everything they need. There are two problems with this.

First, if you're speaking for 90 minutes there is no way you can teach them everything in that time and have it make sense. It's like giving someone the Cliff Notes and expecting them to become an expert on War and Peace. All you'll do is overwhelm and confuse them, and there is one thing that you can be 100% certain a buyer is not going to do if they're overwhelmed and confused: buy.

Second, if you give them everything it's like sitting them at an all-you-can-eat buffet and not letting them get up until it's all gone. They are stuffed. They can't handle another thing. Then you make your pitch and it's like taking them to that supermarket I mentioned at the start of this chapter.

At the other extreme is the speaker who gives nothing, usually because they're afraid that if you give your audience the information they need they'll go away and do it themselves, and they won't buy.

Every audience you speak to will include people who just want the info and they'll go away and try to figure it out themselves. It's the same people who bring a box home from Ikea, dump it on the floor and start assembling their furniture without opening the instructions. Good for them.

The room also has people who want help whatever happens. These are the people who watch a cookery show then order takeout. They watch a DIY show then hire a contractor to fit their kitchen. And there are more than enough of them in your audience to keep you busy!

But here's the thing. If you give your audience too little they can't evaluate what you know. They also don't get a good idea of what's involved. Always give them your best material. Let them see that you know what you're talking about. Trust that they will want more.

Mistake #7. Not Making Them Want It

Mistake 7 is an easy trap to fall into. You know people *need* your product or service, so you assume they *want* it. Unfortunately, human nature being what it is, people tend to want what they don't need, and they don't want what they need. I *need* a car that will get me from A to B, safely and economically. Lots of cars meet those criteria. But I *want* a Tesla Sedan. Not the same thing!

Also, we tend to pay more for the things we want, and less for the things we need. I need an accountant every year to do my books. But I don't wake up thinking "I want an accountant", so I try to find the cheapest option possible.

So before you make your pitch, make them want what you're offering, and make them show it publicly—even if it's just a show of hands.

"Needs" won't get you a six-figure payday. "Wants" will.

Mistake #8. Making The Offer At The Wrong Time

Mistake 8 is the most serious mistake you can make pitching from the stage. Rookie presenters leave the sale to the end of the presentation, when your buyers are thinking about coffee, or getting out of the parking lot before the rush.

Also, at the end of your content there's a feeling of completeness. They've got your seven steps or whatever. They don't need—or want—any more for now.

The expert pitcher will leave part of their content until after the offer, so the audience is still hungry.

Finally, at the end of the content people know the pitch is coming, so they turn off.

If you start early and say, "I mentioned I would talk about how we can continue our journey. Before I share my final points, is it still OK with you if I talk briefly about that?" it makes them curious. I've never had an audience say no! So you're good to make your pitch.

Mistake #9. Not Knowing The Numbers

When I started working with Peter he set me a target: he would fill the room, and for every person in the audience he expected me to make $800 in sales over the course of a weekend. Why that rather than a fixed target? Simple: he knew his numbers.

He knew how much it cost him to get someone into the room and he knew what a customer was worth to him. He also knew what he could have sold making the pitch himself and what other speakers would have sold.

You need to know your numbers too.

I know, because I've tracked my sales, that I can sell $2000 per head in a weekend event: $167 per hour for each person in an audience. It's a number event organisers want to know. It means they can figure out how much money they'll make if they put me on the stage. Of course, it's not guaranteed—it depends on making the right offer to the right audience—but it's worth knowing.

It means I can test changes to my pitches. If I change something and my sales per head goes down I know not to do that in future. If I change something and sales per head goes up, I keep doing it.

So track your numbers. Even if it starts at $10 per person per hour, that's valuable information, and you'll be able to track your improvement.

Bringing it together

As I said before, simply checking that you're not making these mistakes will make a tremendous difference to your presentations. And it doesn't have to be a sales pitch. If you're making a proposal to your boss to get your plan approved, check it exactly the same way: control your state, connect, get permission, tell your story, have the path mapped out, give them just enough content, make them want it, make your request at the right time, and track how often you hear "yes".

I'd like to give you some resources to help improve your sales presentations even further.

> **BONUS**
> To download my "Speak-To-Sell Blueprint"—a one-page, step-by-step map of exactly how to structure your next sales presentation, simply visit http://0s4.com/r/TMITB2.

About the Author

Rob Cuesta is an expert in online brand optimisation, sales funnel acceleration and customer value maximisation, based in Toronto, Canada.

Rob is the owner of Joined-Up Marketing and HyperSuasion Consulting, and author of two Amazon best-selling books on marketing for professionals. With a client base that spans four continents and over 25 years' experience as a speaker, consultant and marketer, Rob has worked with some of the largest organisations in the world and some of the smallest.

"A lot of money gets wasted by businesses every year on marketing that, quite frankly, doesn't work. After completing my MBA at a top European business school I realised that what was missing from a lot of the standard marketing approaches was a way of showing a direct link from marketing to revenue.

Business owners were screaming 'show me the money!' and marketers couldn't. Or wouldn't. So I made myself a promise: to only use marketing techniques—for myself and for my clients—that would directly drive money into the business."

As the creator of the Joined-Up Digital Marketing System, Rob's promise is simple: to help you add an extra zero to your income by positioning you as the leading expert in your field and then developing marketing funnels that convert total strangers into buyers, repeat buyers, and ultimately into referrers. All on autopilot.

WARNING: working with Rob may expose you to revolutionary ideas, untapped revenue streams and extreme profitability. You have been warned!

7 Ways to Profit from Starring in Your Own Show
by Niki Faldemolaei

Imagine yourself as the host of your own show. Who would you model? Would you interview experts or offer advice? Would you play a game or critique other talent? Admit it. There are times when you watch a show and think, "They don't know what they are talking about", or "I can do better". Well, your time has come. It has never been as easy and inexpensive to produce your own show than right now. So what are you waiting for?

Why a show you ask? Let's do an exercise for a minute and reframe what you are doing in your practice. No matter what type of business you have, you are in show business. The business of showing people your skills and knowledge. You are also in the event business. Your success relies upon the events you attend and the people with whom you surround yourself. When you engage with your network of influencers, you automatically get real-time feedback to your offerings, enabling you to tweak and correct as you go. At that point, and only then, it is your engaging content that will attract the biggest brands in the world, including Amazon, Apple, Facebook, Google, LinkedIn, Twitter, and YouTube. These mega-giants will actively promote your engaging offerings and some will even pay you to bring them your content. Back to the show.

Since a single chapter is not enough space to go into detail, a brief overview follows with links to detailed resources. The show, or Livecast, framework can be organized into three parts: the technology, the preparation, and the delivery. You can find the technology buyers guide in the appendix of this book, explaining the platform, software, and studio setup for small, medium, and large budgets. The preparation list and delivery list can be found at http://multicastprofits.com, and will cover slide development, practice-run tips, and pre-show plan, as well as the live event setup, logistics, and after-event process.

The path of least resistance is the ideal way to start. Let's use a healer, Laurie, as our Avatar[1] who has an alternative healing therapy practice in California. Laurie routinely speaks at conferences, hosts a radio show, offers live workshops and sells books, CDs and DVDs. She is an ideal candidate for success because she is an implementer who has hundreds of hours of content that is underutilized! It simply needs to be repurposed for maximized distribution! We will visit 7 Ways to Profit later in this Chapter.

Since video and streaming are mega-trends for billions of users with smartphones and tablets, our first step with Laurie is to start capturing Laurie's audio radio shows with video. YouTube Live and Google Hangouts On Air are free services that enable her to capture her interviews live, share screens, and feature her guests in real time. With a simple adjustment, she can add her existing commercials and sponsors to this live event to monetize her show.

Our strategy is to keep Laurie in motion, tweaking something she already does (turning audio into video), then repurposing and/or adding bonuses with her books, CDs, DVDs and workshops as we map her campaigns to deliver her content everywhere in every format to every device, a strategy known as Multicast Marketing.

For those who do not have a lot of content ready to re-purpose, such as a startup practitioner, I would recommend starting with an interview-style video capture session. Since this individual is an unknown, they might choose to leverage other people's talent and brand recognition.

A real world example of a startup success, ***Entrepreneur on Fire*** Founder John Lee Dumas, discovered the magic when he started interviewing successful business owners about their

---

[1] An Avatar is the perfect customer for your product or service.

strategies and achievements. He started by asking well-known authors and entrepreneurs with recent business success to share their stories and be interviewed on his show. He took the fastest route by interviewing his guests as an audio podcast, blocking out one day per week to capture 7 episodes, launched his daily drive-time podcast, and went on to build a 7-figure empire in 13 months! John generously offers his strategies and resources at http://www.entrepreneuronfire.com.

Another real world example of digitizing shows is the trend where celebrities are moving from TV to Online streaming. Late Night Host Jay Leno, Anchorwoman Katie Couric, and E!'s Chelsea Handler are moving to online shows.

With the onset of mobile devices dominating our attention span, there is huge growth potential for budding entrepreneurs in virtually any industry. Whether you are a healer, coach, or financial maven, you have the opportunity to become the early-adopter of a ridiculously inexpensive business model that is threatening to be the next disruptive technology.[2] Next we will take a look at some creative ways to use the content from your show to achieve multicast profits.

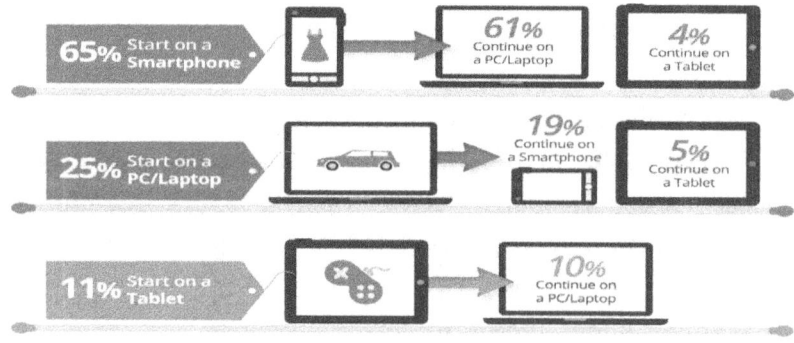

Consumers take a multi-device path to purchase

---

[2] Wiki - disruptive technology is an innovation that helps create a new market and value network, and eventually disrupts an existing market and value network, displacing an earlier technology. An example would be how Netflix and Hulu are displacing Cable TV.

7 Ways to Profit by Starring in Your Own Show

1. **Multicast** – The strategy of creating content once, then repurposing it to reach every device, in every format, delivering content everywhere in the world is referred to as multicast marketing. Your customers want to consume your content in their preferred way, whether it is auditory, visual, or kinesthetic. Creating your multiplatform content and distributing it in multicast outlets gives you the unfair advantage in reaching your target audience. **Your profit lever:** No matter where your customer looks, they can now find properly ranked content that is yours. Over 220 million buyers seek to purchase via Amazon. Over 400 million buyers seek to purchase via Apple Store. There are over 2 billion tablets, 3 billion laptops, and 7 billion smartphones from which people shop and consume engaging content like yours. Leveraging these digital landscapes is vital to business success.

2. **Livecast** – Your show can capture via video and/or broadcast with YouTube Live and Google Hangouts On Air for free with unlimited viewers. This digital technology is replacing analog broadcast, cable, and film. You can now replace radio and TV with free delivery tools connecting to virtually any device, anytime, anywhere. **Your profit lever:**

Utilizing your show with the leverage of your guest's brand is a powerful way to engage your audience in deadline offers, live discounts, and bonuses, each pointing to new and enticing added value offers. Product launches in the Internet marketing worlds have consistently reached million dollar days from a single live event.

3. **Podcast** – This is the most overlooked opportunity in online marketing. Podcasting is as simple as taking your audio, video, and PDF content and distributing it to the 800 lb. gorilla Apple to reach millions of buyers to see your content. **Your profit lever:** Podcasters have surpassed the radio and TV talk show model and turned it into a self-sustaining business with earnings from subscriptions and/or advertising and sponsorships. When your subscribers listen to you on the run, in the car, or on headphones, you have an intimacy of which most marketers can only dream.

17 Secrets from a Marketing Mastermind

4. **Bookcast** – Attaining Author Expert status is a powerful way to position you as an authority to open doors for media interviews, speaking engagements, and consulting gigs. It is as easy as taking your show content, transcribing it, and turning it into a book. The old paradigm where authors hope to make their income from books sales has taken a critical turn toward the creative. **Your profit lever:** Your book is your ticket to partnerships with media events, charitable programs, and corporate endorsements. Offering to give your book away at joint events with relevant brand names elevates your status as an expert. Leveraging these partnerships expands your reach 10x $$$ beyond a traditional book tour. You quickly earn the right to use "As seen on...", adding mega media logos in your promotions.

There's Money in This Book

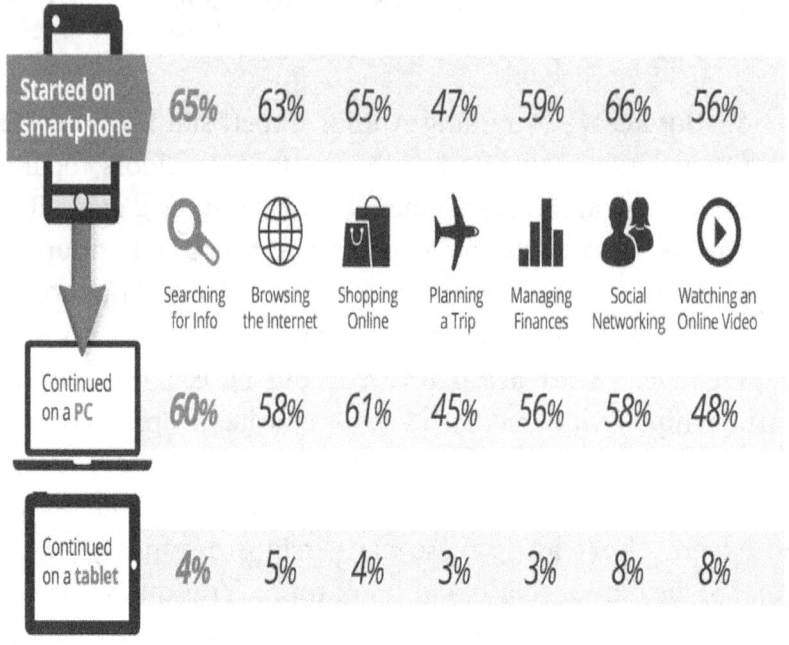

In summary, smartphones are the backbone of our daily media interactions. They have the highest number of user interactions per day and serve as the most common starting point for activities across multiple screens.

Businesses need to consider:

- Adjusting conversion goals to account for the differences in end user goals when using each device.

- Tailoring the user experience to each device to account for the differences in how users shop.

Going mobile has become a business imperative.

5. **Mobilecast** – A mind-blowing 7 billion mobile accounts exist (= number of world population) making the mobile delivery market the most dynamic potential for growth.[3] Soon,

texting, SMS, and scanning QR codes will be standard procedure for gathering leads from live events and networking circles. **Your profit lever:** Since sales are dependent on your list, the mobile capture of leads has a direct impact on revenue. Most Futurists will agree that mobile commerce is one of the most important trends of this time. You are in the right place at the right time to put your content in the pockets of billions. Seize it!

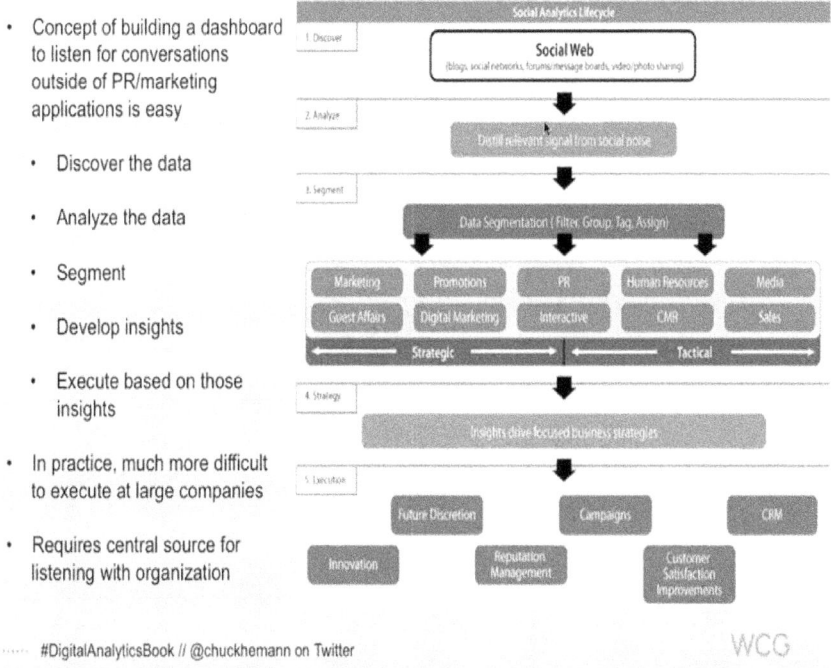

6. **Socialcast** – Syndication of your content is key to building your brand and your income. You can now cater to your audience on their terms, where they spend their time. You might reach a celebrity on Twitter or a business colleague on LinkedIn. Whether your audience is blogging or watching

---

[3] http://www.itu.int/en/ITU-D/Statistics/Documents/facts/ICTFactsFigures2014-e.pdf

YouTube videos, they will find you. **Your profit lever:** Engagement of your audience through bonus offers puts them into a queue where you give them high quality, meaningful content over time to build trust, followed by the conversion to sales after 3, 7, or 12 interactions with you.

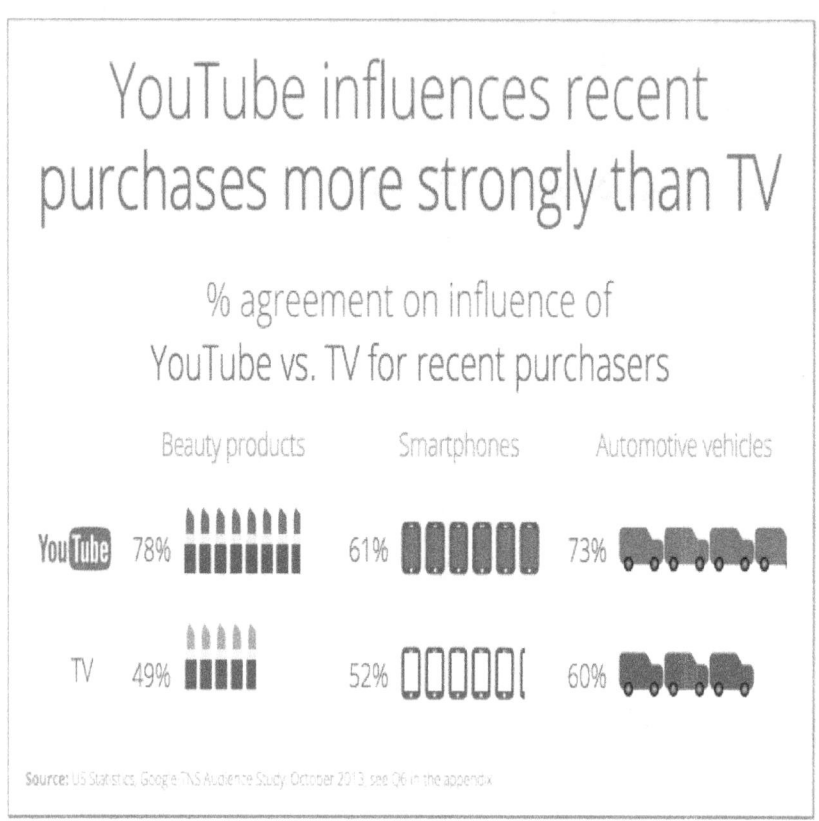

7. **Broadcast** – You may have heard the prediction that Cable is dying thanks in part to Netflix, Hulu, and Amazon Prime. As markets shift from analog to digital delivery, media organizations are scrambling to stay current while their programming and operations are disrupted by the onset of iTV, tablets, and smartphones as the preferred way to watch shows. **Your profit lever:** This is a perfect time for your show to be that trend, or to become a consultant to celebrities, casting

directors, writers, and producers for TV/Film. You may be a technology consultant or an expert in a specific role or show idea. Digitizing your content and positioning yourself as an expert in your field gives you an unfair advantage. Get there first!

> **BONUS**
> To receive a free Livecast monetization map visit http://LeadWithLivecast.com

About the Author

Author of *Lead With Livecast, The Complete Blueprint to Monetizing Your Speaking Gigs, Workshops and Teaching Content.* As a Marketing and Technology Consultant, Niki provides strategic direction in Life Science, media, education, manufacturing, distribution, and sales organizations. She creates global awareness programs and facilitates enterprise solutions to transition from high-quality print and traditional education outlets into the digital world of new media and multi-device delivery.

Niki served 20 years in corporate biotechnology and new media industries followed by 10 years in entrepreneurial product and service launches, campaigns utilizing cutting-edge intelligence, and live event promotions for celebrity athletes and pioneering healers.

While working with Newspaper Association of America, IMG Creative, and Proelite, Niki achieved successful client placements in USA Today, Newsweek, Washington Post, NY Times, Huffington Post, Muscle & Fitness, Cannes Film Festival, Toronto Film Festival, Sundance Channel, National Geographic Channel, and Showtime. Niki also earned agency, publishing and NY Times interactive awards.

- Author Expert Marketing Machines Certified Expert
- Multicast Marketing Machines Training
- Instant Customer Mastery Certified Expert
- Top Gun Consulting Toolkit Certified Consultant
- Instant Customer Reinvention Training
- Publish & Profit Certification

Visit Niki at http://TempleArtsCommunications.com, receive a free Livecast monetization map visit http://LeadWithLivecast.com, and view Livecast resources at http://MulticastProfits.com

Disclaimer: Results not typical. We are not lawyers or CPAs and recommend you check in with your own counsel when choosing to engage in this new world of marketing technology.

Images: Multicast and Mobilecast images by http://www.keepitusable.com/blog/?p=493, Podcast Image by John Lee Dumas

Go from Marketing Frustration to Marketing Sensation: 7 Steps to a Successful Crowd Grabber Campaign
by Karol H. Clark, MSN, RN

Have you ever felt as if you were paying for marketing mediocrity? Have you ever felt as if you were working REALLY hard and getting nowhere fast? Have you ever woke up in the middle of the night, fearful of what was going to happen to you, your family, and/or your business as a result of uncertain economic times? Do you love what you do and love helping others, but are frustrated by your inability to get your message out to the masses and finally experience financial freedom?

If you answered yes to any of these questions, you have bought the right book and you are in the right place at the right time! You are about to be connected in a BIG way!

I can honestly say that my husband and I experienced all of the feelings listed above—particularly in 2011 and still sometimes today. We are pioneers in the field of surgical and medical weight loss. We love providing services in a unique way that exceed patient expectations and have been doing this for well over 20 years. As the only bariatric surgeon in the state of Virginia not owned by a large health system, some feel as if my husband is crazy and others think he is a genius, and they strive to duplicate our successful model. Now we even help others do just that!

If you are reading this book, you are likely a pioneer and entrepreneur yourself. You can understand the desire to be independent...to do things in a unique way...to exceed your customers' expectations...to truly LOVE what you do...to control your destiny...and to help others look/feel/BE their BEST in life and/or business. That's what makes us happy. That's what keeps entrepreneurs like us going!

But let's be real. For us, as an independent practice, we don't have deep pockets for radio/TV advertising. We hang our hat on creating a tribe of successful, happy patients who refer family, friends, and acquaintances from local areas and around the world to us as well. Unfortunately, if you aren't constantly reaching out to grow your ubiquity footprint and acquiring new leads who want/need your services, you may not survive and thrive as you had hoped and planned.

At the Center for Weight Loss Success, we like providing concierge services to motivated people who want long-term weight loss success. We enjoy surrounding ourselves with a quality, self-directed team that is passionate and shares our vision. They represent us and are crucial to our success. They are family to us. We also like operating "out of the box" while being "by the book" when it comes to business. We like to provide a pleasant, unexpected warm touch when it comes to customer service. We also like to have fun! However, we are not your typical "marketers". We are clinicians.

So what could we do? Well, in 2011, we opened a new center in Newport News, VA. It is 10,000 square feet and within these inviting walls, we provide surgical weight loss and non-surgical weight loss services, operate a nutritional store filled with great tasting supplements/pharmaceutical grade vitamins and a state-of-the-art fitness center.

We made a HUGE investment to open this center and quite frankly, it was somewhat scary! We wanted to offer everything someone needs for successful weight loss under one roof in a warm, motivating and safe environment. We never wanted to wake up one day realizing we never fulfilled this dream. However, the investment was steep and we needed to not only survive, but thrive in this uncertain healthcare environment.

Prior to opening our new facility, we hired a local marketing expert we knew and liked who was great. She and her team helped us build our new brand that replaced our past separate medical, surgical, and fitness offices. We had a unique grand opening that people wrote articles about and still talk about today. Our new name, our new facility, our continuing dream was off and running...slowly. Changing the name was confusing to many people, but the right thing to do in the long run. In fact, we had many sleepless nights worrying about being able to keep up. Marketing expenses were high. Patients were happy, but we needed a better marketing return on investment (ROI). We knew we could do anything we set our minds to (just as we teach our four children). We buckled down and began to master the most cost-effective marketing out there...online marketing. It was the right move. We have never looked back and love it!

Now, we and our team have four Amazon best-selling books (and more on the way). We also implemented a robust online membership program, two free weekly podcast series, active Facebook, Pinterest, LinkedIn, blog, Google+ and Twitter pages, referral programs, free programs for the community, and monthly events that reward our patients—all of which we created in the past two years!

But the activity that feeds it all is what I am going to address in this chapter—our effective lead generation strategy using Crowd Grabber Campaigns, which can be used by anyone, anywhere, in any business. Follow these 7 Steps to a Successful Crowd Grabber Campaign and you will be on your way to an enjoyable, sustainable business.

So what's a Crowd Grabber Campaign you might ask? Where did it come from? Better yet, how can it help you?

Well, in 2012, I was at the peak of my frustration with marketing. We had so many strategies in place and yet, our ROI was marginal at best. We felt as if we were working REALLY hard with minimal return.

One weekend afternoon, I found myself immersed in an online "infomercial" by Mike Koenigs (www.MikeKoenigs.com). He was talking directly to me. He seemed to understand my frustration and I listened to him for well over 10 minutes (rare for me). Even more amazing, he wasn't offensive. He was likable, extremely confident, and sincere. He was offering a solution that sounded too good to be true (as long as I committed to learning and implementing his tools). Well, I was eager, excited, and up for the challenge! He made his offer a "no-brainer" and I quickly bought into his system. Not only his system, but hands-on training that I absorbed like a sponge and "the rest is history" so to speak. The key is discipline and implementation. Anyone who knows me understands that is a part of my DNA—thanks Mom and Dad! Fortunately, it is even more so for my husband. He is the visionary and I tend to be the "go-to" gal. In addition, we believe in surrounding ourselves with high-quality people who share our passion and vision.

Since that time, we have been exposed to some of Mike's colleagues such as Pam Henderson, Ed Rush, and Paul Colligan. I have become certified in some of their products, participated in the creation of one of their programs, and made more trips to San Diego than me or my family ever imagined possible! I have met the most wonderful and talented people (many of whom are co-authors in this book) and implemented in a bigger way than ever imaginable. One of Mike Koenigs' tools is Instant Customer with its infamous "Crowd Grabber Campaign" which is the focus of this chapter since it is hands down one of the most effective things you can do for your business—I know it has been for ours and for so many others.

The Crowd Grabber Campaign is a way for you to capture leads anytime and anywhere. Does that sound too good to be true? Well, I will share with you my 7 Steps to a Successful Crowd Grabber Campaign within Instant Customer (www.instantcustomer.com) and provide access to several campaign examples I have built in literally five minutes that have resulted in much greater exposure, enabling us to help so many more people.

Also, it has added significant revenue to our bottom line and helped me successfully launch three additional businesses (Weight Loss Practice Builder, Center for Hormone Health and Wellness, and Your Best Seller Book). Don't just take my word for it—every author in this book is adept at creating an effective Crowd Grabber Campaign in about five minutes and has numerous examples to share. You can do the same...whether you want to learn it yourself or hire someone experienced to "work the magic" for your marketing ROI, you can make this work for your business. Let's get to it!

7 Steps to a Successful Crowd Grabber Campaign

1. Understand and Harness the Power of a Crowd Grabber Campaign

Whether you want to acquire potential leads at a trade show, dinner meeting, teleseminar, webinar, livecast, group presentation, a chance encounter, print/online advertisement, storefront, on your business card, or within any of your social media sites as you sleep, the Instant Customer Crowd Grabber Campaign is your answer. Your prospective leads can subscribe to your campaign literally anywhere, anytime, and on any device. I don't know about you, but I think that is pretty powerful! This campaign had me from "hello" and I use it all the time for our businesses (examples included in Step 3).

This technology is perfect for anyone who is an experienced marketer/designer or for those of us who know what we want/need/like for our business or our clients' businesses, but don't want to have to go back to school to earn your graphic design or computer engineering degree. We want to either easily do it ourselves or hire someone who can create what we want quickly and tweak it along the way as necessary based upon campaign results. Let's face it...results are what matter most—not just creating a pretty campaign.

Your subscriber list will grow much more quickly if you offer multiple ways to opt-in. At your fingertips (within Instant Customer), you have the ability to instantly create all of the following:

- *Lead Capture Flyer* that automatically includes opt-in methods including text (SMS long code AND short code you specify), phone (you can choose local number or toll-free number), QR code, and a website URL you reserve within Instant Customer or through the third-party vendor of your choice (i.e. BlueHost or GoDaddy). This is perfect for speaking engagements, trade shows, or any brick-and-mortar business.
- *Mobile Optimized Lead Capture Website* so that your leads can opt-in on any device. Optimized means that coding for your site is complete (here it has already been done for you) to ensure that your site will format perfectly to whatever device the user is viewing it on. I don't know about you, but I am not a coder and knowing that this is done for me makes me very happy! This is critical in an environment where most websites are not optimized and yet sites are viewed regularly on a mobile device...you have likely experienced this yourself. This is perfect for literally every business today.
- *Auto-Responder Follow-Up Messages* so you can deliver what you may have promised (i.e., bonus report, video, or book), continue to nurture your relationship, and share your specific call to action. Your follow-up messages can include additional website links, video, PDF attachments—the sky is the limit. If someone opts-in via text (SMS) message, and did not include their e-

mail, the system automatically sends them a text message asking for it. It doesn't get much easier than that. Also, within the system (for non-marketers or those that don't want to re-invent the wheel), there are sample messages included to guide you every step of the way. The legal requirements for opting-in to your campaign and methods for opting-out are included as well.

Remember, people buy when *they* are ready. You want to be the one in front of them when they decide to buy. A follow-up/nurturing sequence is a great way to do that without being annoying. Provide quality content to them on a regular (well-spaced) basis. Be true to your cause and ethically sound. Your prospects will begin to know, like, and trust you and you will be their likely choice when they are ready to buy. As a warning, you MUST include your call to action; otherwise, they may never "pull the trigger" with you to buy and experience all you have to offer. Auto-responders can work effectively for any business when done correctly.

I hope you are sensing the power you have at your fingertips. Read on now for "how to" harness this power in your particular business— no matter what your business may be.

2. Be Clear About the Purpose of Your Crowd Grabber Campaign (Your Desired Outcome)

It's easy to do repetitive, non-productive tasks because that's what you are used to doing. You may be too overwhelmed and too busy to even realize it. Of course, that's another entire book on planning, organizing, and time management. The reality is that you need to ask yourself, "Is what I am doing right now getting me closer to where I want to be tomorrow?" If the answer is "no", then you need to reconsider your actions. This is true in weight loss, fitness, relationships, and business. It's true for literally every aspect of your life and particularly when it comes to your marketing strategies.

Before you begin, you need to ask yourself, "What is the purpose of this campaign? What is my desired outcome?" You also need to be specific. If you are working with a consultant, he/she will ask you this from the very beginning.

Keeping your desired outcome top-of-mind will ensure that you create a much more effective campaign and help to eliminate unnecessary frustration. Use of this easy Instant Customer Crowd Grabber technology also makes your efforts cost effective (and we're just scratching the surface of everything Instant Customer can do for you). Some common goals of a crowd grabber campaign are to:

- Capture leads for purchase and/or promotion of your new book
- Capture leads for a new or existing business venture
- Capture leads for a specific advertising campaign you are running
- Capture leads who have read your book and are hungry for more of your information/products/services
- Capture leads from a specific event

No matter what the reason, this purpose/goal will guide your design and messaging for the videos, banner and text you create for your campaign materials and follow-up auto-responder messages.

3. Plan Your Campaign

"If you fail to plan, you are planning to fail!"...Benjamin Franklin

Such wise words from a wise man and yet planning is often overlooked. Instead, in today's fast-paced society, many times "action" is taken before thinking through the consequences. The most efficient use of time, energy, and resources to meet the desired outcome are rarely considered...let alone what the goal is in the first place! There is never enough time to do it right, but always enough time to do it over. So why not take the time to do it right the first time?

When setting up a Crowd Grabber Campaign, you will be doing yourself a favor if you use the set-up questionnaire within Instant Customer. This will make creating your campaign from either the Express Set-Up or Customized Set-Up templates a breeze. However, if you jump right in without remembering the big picture, some of the questions won't make as much sense. It is important to stay true to your purpose, try not to be intimidated or overwhelmed, and ask for help if you need it. The tool is truly turnkey, but if you are like me, sometimes use of a new tool can be daunting, until I actually do it myself or walk through the process with someone else a time or two.

Remember that you don't necessarily have to use all of the media sources provided, but just know they are available and easy to use. To help demonstrate, I will share a step-by-step planning process below which includes specific information from an active "Your Best Seller Book" Crowd Grabber Campaign I created. For your convenience, I also included several additional samples from other successful Crowd Grabber Campaigns at the end of this planning section.

This particular Crowd Grabber campaign is for a joint venture I created with the publisher for our three consecutive Amazon Best-Selling books published within the last year. We found that we had a positive, natural working relationship and complementary talents. I enjoy project management, content creation, content organization for optimal flow, editing, and marketing. She enjoys editing, creating book titles and covers, researching categories on Amazon, creating author pages on Amazon, managing hard-copy production, coordinating the launch, tracking launch progress/results, and keeping books top of mind after getting to #1. We both love the rush of getting a book to an Amazon best-seller status (16 consecutive non-fiction Amazon best-sellers in 2013 alone). After all of this success, we decided to launch this joint venture to help even more authors. A Crowd Grabber Campaign has been the perfect venue to do just that.

First, determine your desired outcome. *This helps you keep a clear picture of your goals and a benchmark for overall campaign success.* We desire to publish (quality over quantity) 10-15 high-quality, non-fiction best-selling books/year for motivated, goal-oriented, successful professionals who have a valuable message to share with their ideal clients. Although we could have developed a more complicated funnel with trip-wires and other methodology, we decided to keep it simple (which is often better since too many options often leads to prospect 'overwhelm' and indecision, which results in lower opt-in and purchase rates).

Second, investigate the pain points or greatest needs of your ideal clients. *This will drive the messaging copy for your crowd grabber campaign.* For us, this includes about four primary scenarios. This also drives which sales package we offer that might be most appropriate for them when the right time comes for that introduction. In the meantime, we will focus on providing them with quality information (it's always good to under-promise and over-deliver). The scenarios include:

- A professional who just needs their existing written materials organized and published.
- A professional who has a draft of their manuscript in hand and is ready to take the next steps of editing and publishing.

- A professional who is starting from scratch and needs assistance with all of the moving parts of manuscript creation and publishing.
- A professional who meets any of the above criteria and wants to dominate their market, crush their competition, and be identified as the expert in their industry.

Third, map out your lead capture funnel from initial opt-in, your "free offer" (sometimes called an ethical bribe), or bonus that will entice prospects to join, your auto responder follow-up sequence, and sales offers. *This keeps you focused on what you want your prospect to do.* For us, our funnel included various ways to drive traffic to our lead capture page (speaking engagements, business cards, use of the Crowd Grabber flyer, QR code, and other marketing efforts not covered in this particular chapter), opt-in, delivery of free resources as promised (videos/action guide, checklist), follow-up sequence, personalized consultation and sale of one of our publishing packages as appropriate.

Fourth, we determined what resources we needed to create prior to creating the campaign. *Having this done ahead of time keeps you organized and makes a 5-minute Crowd Grabber Campaign build realistic.* For us, this included our banner for the webpage, a professional photo with both of us, a quick opt-in video, a quick thank-you video and our free giveaway (5 videos and Step-by-Step Quick-Start Action Guide). These can be viewed/obtained at www.YourBestSellerBook.com. Often, you will have your free giveaway (if applicable) already created and ready to go (i.e., book for promotion, free report or simple checklist) which will decrease your preparation time.

Finally, we answered the Instant Crowd Grabber Campaign template worksheet questions so we would have everything ready to go as I built the campaign within Instant Customer. You can obtain additional information and a sample of the questionnaire from Instant Customer at www.instantcrowdgrabber.com I recommend typing the answers and having the document open in front of you when you build your campaign so you can easily copy and paste the information right into the campaign builder within Instant Customer.

4. Create Any Necessary Media

If you followed the steps outlined thus far, you will know exactly what you need to create. Do not make necessary media creation too difficult. Do not overthink it. You do not have to break the bank either. Here are the basic items you need to have ready to upload into Instant Customer:

- Header Image which will be placed in the header of all of your pages. It can be a banner or your logo. The maximum width is 800 pixels and the recommended size is 800 W x 225 H.
- Consultant (your) photo which will be placed in the "about us" section of all of your pages. The maximum width is 200 pixels and the recommended size is 200 W x 225 H.
- Opt-in video (various sizes accepted) which will automatically play on your lead page when prospects arrive to your page from one of your MANY Crowd Grabber opt-in methods. The focus of this chapter is not to teach you video techniques, but take it from me; you can make this as hard or easy as you want (but let's keep it simple). The most important thing is your message—be brief and to the point. This is where you thank them for visiting your page and give them a reason to opt-in on the page. This is usually to promote your bonus. It's amazing how easy video has become through the use of iPhones or reasonably priced cameras. You can see

some sample pages from Crowd Grabber Campaigns we created that have converted well which we created on an iPhone at
www.weightlosssuccess4me.com;
www.myweightlosssurgerysuccess.com;
www.yoursurgeryprep.com;
www.weightlossforfarmers.com and
www.yourbestsellerbook.com

- Thank you video (optional) that runs as soon as someone opts-in.

5. Log-In, Upload, and Create!

Now the fun part! Don't stress—there are tutorials and assistance every step of the way within Instant Customer. Not to mention the availability of a help desk, forum of helpful users and certified consultants that can walk through the process with you or do it for you if you prefer.

Log into your account and find "Media Center" under MANAGE in the upper right corner. This is where you will add the files (Video, Audio, Documents, and Images) into your account. This chapter is not a tutorial for Instant Customer, but suffice it to say that the program is intuitive. You will select which type of media you are uploading and then follow the prompts/instructions. All of your media needs to be uploaded before you begin building your Crowd Grabber Campaign.

Have the answers to your questionnaire pulled up on your computer so that you can copy and paste from it easily. Now click on the "Create from Template" under CAMPAIGN. You will see a number of campaign templates. You can search for the Crowd Grabber or just enter "Crowd Grabber" into the search field and enter. You will see it show up right away. Click on the template and follow instructions. The questions within the online campaign template will mirror your questionnaire.

Once you have everything entered, you can go to the webpage within the "edit" portion of your named campaign and make edits in real time. You can do the same with your flyer and any thank you page or auto-responders you create. Here is a sample of the flyer created within our Crowd Grabber campaign for Your Best Seller Book:

17 Secrets from a Marketing Mastermind

Want to Become a Best Selling Author?

5 Simple Steps for Your Quick Success Yours FREE along with access to two experts with 16 consecutive #1 best-selling books in 2013 alone!

Enroll now and you'll receive:

- Five Free Videos and a Must-Have Action Guide that teaches you:
    - How to resonate with your ideal audience
    - Easy ways to overcome fears you may have
    - Simple strategies for creating your book in as little as 2 days
    - Steps to successfully publishing your book
    - How to quickly get your to best-seller status
- Summary of Your Various Publishing Options and Insider Terms You Need to Know
  Our publishing expert guides you through the maze of book distribution options without breaking the bank!
- A list of common book publishing mistakes and how to avoid them
  Want to see the final result? We'll give you access to the finished product.

And much more!

Instantly join by using one of the methods on the right.

Don't delay - it's easier than you think!

Register now to receive

Five free videos and a must have action guide so you can turn your knowledge into revenue in as little as 4-6 weeks!

BY MOBILE SMS:
Text your name and email to
+1 (214) 717-4999

SCAN THIS QR CODE

OR VISIT THIS WEB PAGE
www.YourBestSellerBook.com

YOUR BEST-SELLER BOOK

As with anything new, there is a learning curve. However, I can honestly say that this tool is well worth the learning curve. Also, the resources for assistance are abundant and the time you put in will provide a plentiful return when executed properly.

6. Test/Edit

You MUST view/test/edit prior to "going live". This involves going to your page and making sure that you like the look, flow, colors, and content layout. You also need to test your funnel/opt-in and have a few other people test it as well. This is time well spent. You want the experience of your prospective clients to be as perfect as possible (realizing that few if any online systems work perfect every time).

If you have edits to make, log into your account, select your campaign and click "edit". You can then go to the "builder" and make real time edits. Once you have your campaign and flyer looking the way you want, just save—then you are ready to rock and roll!

7. Promote/Put Into Action/Prosper

Here's where the rubber meets the road! It's exciting, it's sometimes frustrating, and it's your future! Seriously, why put so much effort into creating your Crowd Grabber Campaign without promoting it so you get the results you want/deserve? This is the part where I have to really focus. I love creating, but I am a clinician at heart. I like to help people and I am not very comfortable "promoting". My clinical side wants to give everything away and that's not a very viable way to do business. It took me a while to get over the fact that promotion is a GOOD thing—not a pompous, annoying, or selfish thing to do. It is a very important part of business.

What helped me is realizing that by promoting myself, my husband, our awesome services and staff, along with other quality people/businesses, I am actually helping more people through a much wider reach. There is not a shortage of business, especially if you focus on your ideal clients, provide quality content/services, and treat others well. What you really do then is create a tribe of people who actually want MORE from you and look forward to what you offer next. It is also imperative to surround yourself with people who are positive and share your passion. Be sure to treat them well too. This includes your colleagues, your employees, your vendors, and all who are like minded. Being an entity unto yourself doesn't work very well. Build networks, learn from others, and help them learn from you. The financial return will be amazing and life will be much more enjoyable. Promote with sincerity, follow through, and you will prosper.

Your Crowd Grabber Campaign is created. What do you do next? You need to promote it so you can build your list of interested, qualified leads! Here's what you do (feel free to implement any/all of these strategies—many are explained thoroughly in the other chapters within this book:

- If you have Instant Customer (or your consultant is using Instant Customer) then you/they likely have access to Traffic Geyser (another Mike Koenigs' tool). It's a one-stop-shop for getting—well, you know—traffic! One upload, keyword optimization, one click, and your information is out on major social media sites instantly.
- Search out public speaking engagements where your ideal clients are and put that flyer to use!
- Share your Crowd Grabber Campaign within the Instant Customer member's only site and you will be amazed at the support/shares you will receive.

- Add your campaign URL to your business card and hand it out!
- Join groups where your customers are and share your quality information/campaign link with them.
- Begin a cost-effective Facebook Campaign
- Use your Crowd Grabber at your booth in a trade show or local event
- Don't forget to read all of the chapters in this book. Many address how to maximize promotion of your campaign through social media (Facebook, Twitter, Google+, Pinterest, trade shows)
- Split test your offers and tweak your campaigns for optimal results
- Go to live events and share your campaign information via your business card or flyer

So what was this all about? Not just helping others, but prospering as well! Make sure you have your services/products set up in an easy way for purchase. Now that you have planned, created, promoted, tweaked/modified, and reached your ideal audience, it is time to over-deliver, build your tribe, and…you've got it…PROSPER!

I wish you much happiness, health, success, and prosperity. As my husband always says…"Life is what we do minute to minute and day to day. Remember to enjoy the journey along the way." If I can be of any assistance, please do not hesitate to contact me at karol@weightlosspracticebuilder.com

About the Author

Karol Clark is formally trained as master's prepared Registered Nurse in the field of women's health, medical and surgical weight loss, and nutrition. Karol is also a marketing expert with over 20 years of experience as a hospital administrator, surgical practice administrator, and consultant. Karol has helped her husband, Dr. Thomas W. Clark, create and launch four Amazon best-selling books. She has also helped him integrate successful non-traditional medical marketing strategies such as podcasting, product development, webinars, and membership sites into his busy bariatric surgery practice. Karol utilizes these skills to help other professionals attract the clients they want, become best-selling authors, and grow their practice while enjoying the journey along the way. Karol is also the founder and CEO of *Weight Loss Practice Builder* where she, her husband and her team assist physicians, healthcare practitioners, and fitness professionals to integrate a profitable turnkey weight loss program into their practice. Karol is a certified professional with Author Expert Marketing Machines and Make Market Launch. She lives in Virginia with her husband and their four children. You can reach Karol via LinkedIn or through any of her business sites: www.CFWLS.com, www.WeightLossPracticeBuilder.com, www.YourBestSellerBook.com and www.CenterforHormoneHealthandWellness.com

Reach Your Perfect Audience—Leverage the Power of Facebook Advertising to Target Your Ideal Market
by Dave Pittman

There is no question that Facebook plays a unique role in the ever-connected world in which we live, and has firmly cemented itself in a prominent place within the annals of Internet history. From its humble beginnings in a dorm room at Harvard, to its storied rise and rapid growth up to our present time, Facebook has become the largest, most dominant social networking platform online today.

If you are among the one-fifth of the world's population who has an account on Facebook and uses it at least once a month, then you need no introduction to how it has shaped the way we share, engage, communicate, and stay connected with our family and friends, irrespective of time zone, location, or distance. For better (or worse!), Facebook is here to stay for the long haul, and if you haven't done so already, it's time to seriously consider what role it can and <u>should</u> play in your business and marketing strategy.

Where do you stand?

As you read this, does one of these descriptions apply to you? You currently only use Facebook on a personal level and have yet to consider it for your business. Or perhaps you do have a Facebook business page, but you are confused and overwhelmed by all the advice out there on how to use it effectively, so you don't give it much attention anymore or have simply given up. Or maybe you have a fairly active and well-established Facebook page with plenty of followers (perhaps even thousands or tens of thousands), and you are committed to posting on a regular basis and applying the latest tips and strategies from the social media experts you follow. But despite these efforts, you're *still* not seeing an increase in conversions and sales you were hoping for; or an increase in leads, subscribers, and traffic to your website; and you have challenges growing your audience and expanding your reach beyond your existing followers.

Who this is for

If you fall into any one of the above categories or somewhere in between, do not despair. I have good news!

If you are an

- entrepreneur or business owner of any type, industry, or size
- author, speaker, coach, consultant, or professional of any kind
- blogger, hobbyist, artist, creative type, or individual with a passion

And you have a product, service, or message you want to share with the entire world, or only to the smallest and narrowest of niches — in other words, *YOUR perfect audience* — then there is no better platform right now than Facebook to get your message out there and to use paid advertising as the medium to reach your market.

What You Will Learn

While a single chapter can't cover the entire topic of Facebook advertising from A to Z, we do have three primary objectives:

1) Make the case for paid advertising vs. free traffic alone,

2) Answer the question "Why Facebook?" as an advertising platform and why you shouldn't ignore it, and
3) Dive deep into the heart of what sets Facebook apart: audience targeting.

You will be amazed at the richness of data and level of granularity available to identify and target your perfect audience (hence, the title and focus of this chapter!) and by the time you finish reading, I trust you will be very excited and full of new ideas about how you can apply this for your business.

Finally, given the many components necessary to running a successful advertising campaign that can't be covered here, we're going to give you access to free resources at the end on how to get started and take the next steps. Are you ready to dive in? Let's go!

The Case for Paid Advertising

While much can be said about the topic of "free traffic", the many ways to getting it, and the myths and realities around how easy or effective it actually is, there is no doubt that paid media is still the fastest and most efficient way to put yourself, your products, or services in front of an audience. This is true whether we are talking about search engines, content marketing, video, or any specific social media platform. Since our topic is Facebook, let's specifically focus on that.

Consider again the best of our scenarios mentioned above — you've spent much time, effort, and focus on building your Facebook page and have seen great results. Yet over the past few months, despite your best efforts at continually creating compelling content and staying engaged with your fans, you've seen a dramatic *decrease* in your organic reach lately without any wrongdoing on your part. You're left scratching your head wondering why. You are not alone, as thousands of other frustrated page owners have expressed similar sentiments.

On this point the verdict is in. Facebook has publicly stated that organic reach — that is, how many people you can reach for free by posting to your page — is down. There are two main reasons for this and the first is simple math. More and more content is being created and shared every day, and the total number of pages liked by the typical Facebook user grew more than 50% last year. As a result, with each new page like, there's more competition in the News Feed for your attention. Facebook states,

> *"There is now far more content being made than there is time to absorb it. On average, there are 1,500 stories that could appear in a person's News Feed each time they log on to Facebook. For people with lots of friends and Page likes, as many as 15,000 potential stories could appear any time they log on."*

Fifteen-hundred stories, let alone 15,000?! And you thought your email inbox was out of control! The second reason is that their algorithm is designed to look at thousands of different factors to prioritize and decide which content is most relevant to you. Of those 1500+ stories, the News Feed will only display approximately 300. The bottom line is that for most of the posts you make to your business page, only a small percentage of them will actually appear in your fans and followers' News Feeds.

While organic content still has great value and there are ways to improve your organic reach, the new reality is that just like radio, TV, newspapers, search, and virtually every other marketing platform, you'll reach broader audiences more predictably and with greater accuracy when you use paid media to reach your goals. In other words, you must "pay to play".

Why Facebook

Now that we've made a case for paid advertising, let's look at why Facebook is such a powerful platform, starting with some impressive numbers that paint a pretty compelling picture.

First, Facebook has a massive reach with over 1.3 billion active monthly users. While this clearly makes it the largest social media platform right now, far surpassing other social networks like Google Plus, LinkedIn and Twitter, its audience size alone does not necessarily make it unique. YouTube and Google search each have 1 billion and 1.1 billion unique monthly users, respectively. But what *does* make Facebook stand out is how active and engaged its audience is: 829 million users visit **every single day**. In the US alone, Americans spend an average of 40 minutes per day on Facebook, and when you look at the hours spent per person per month, Facebook clocks in at a total of 6 hours, 35 minutes! This is almost double the time spent on Google (3 hours, 20 minutes) and over 300% longer than Yahoo or Microsoft properties. And that's just on the desktop! Now consider mobile: 654 million daily mobile users, growing at a 61% year over year rate. And of these users, 399 million are exclusively mobile. In other words, about 30% of all Facebook users *only* log in from a smartphone or tablet. Later, we'll highlight why this is relevant and how you can use this strategically inside ad campaigns.

In summary, with an average of over 4.5 billion daily likes, 4.8 billion daily shares, and 12 billion messages sent every single day by up to one fifth of the world's population, Facebook gives you the power to connect with, engage, and influence your customers and reach more people, on more devices, more often than anywhere else. Now that's impressive!

But what if your audience isn't "the world", and you are not a billion-dollar global brand trying to reach the masses?

Perhaps you are a hobbyist, blogger, or solopreneur with an online business in a specific niche; an entrepreneur, coach, or consultant serving a particular industry; a service or health professional trying to target their ideal clientele; or a small business owner of a brick-and-mortar shop trying to expand their reach to more people within their neighborhood or city. This is where Facebook really begins to shine.

Facebook comes with an incredibly powerful set of targeting capabilities that are unmatched by any other advertising platform. It can use the profile information and demographics of every user on its network, along with their behaviors, interests, actions, and activities taken throughout the site (and as we'll see later, even their activities *off* site). Think for a moment about your own personal use of Facebook and what information you share publicly or privately with friends. Now think about all the pages you've liked, the comments you've made, the groups you've joined, the posts you've shared, the places you've checked into, the links you've clicked, the events you've attended, the apps you've downloaded, or the videos you've watched over time — and then multiply that by over one billion people! All of this builds a rich tapestry of data that not only can advertisers tap into to place relevant and tailored ads before you, but *you* — the business owner — can leverage this very same information to create highly selective and targeted campaigns, customizing ads to specific segments of your market, and ultimately reaching your perfect audience.

Even more, when you use a "page post" style ad that appears in the News Feed, it can not only look like a normal post (with images, video, links, and text) and thus feel "less like" an ad, but your ad can be liked, commented on, and shared! You gain the benefit of social proof (which strengthens trust and credibility, and increases sales) *and* the ability for your ad to reach even more people through the engagement actions of your audience. Simply put, fans make your ads more effective, and the social context of likes and shares signal a positive quality of the ad, which leads to better and more efficient auction prices. These are powerful benefits not available anywhere else. We will cover these targeting capabilities in greater detail in the next section.

Finally, let's briefly talk about the advertising landscape on Facebook. With over $2.6 billion in advertising revenue in its most recent quarter and growing at over 41% per year, Facebook is in a strong second position behind Google in worldwide ad revenue, and far ahead of any other competitors. It is not our intention in this chapter nor is there adequate space to provide a Google vs. Facebook comparison or detailed breakdown. In reality, both platforms provide unique advertising advantages and in many cases, it may be appropriate for a business to pursue both.

There are, however, many data points in Facebook's favor that are worth highlighting. In general, Facebook CPC (cost per click) ads are cheaper than Google CPC ads. Facebook has a 35% lower cost per conversion than the online average, and in a recent analysis of over 60 campaigns, 70% of companies had a return of 300% or more on ad spend, and 49% had a 500% or greater ROI! And according to Nielsen, most online advertising reaches only 38% of its intended audience, whereas Facebook's average is a whopping 89%.

In summary, Facebook has the massive reach, unparalleled targeting capabilities, socially endorsable ads, complete mobile and cross-platform integration, is affordable to get started, and has a consistently higher return on ad spend. It has the power to connect, engage, influence, and drive business results. What's not to like?

Target Audience Selection

Now that we've established why Facebook is such a promising advertising platform, let's examine one of its key features in greater depth — target audience selection. As mentioned, Facebook collects a wealth of data starting with basic demographic information that users are willing to share about themselves — age, gender, where they live, etc. This is further enriched by users' interests, behaviors, and connections. As you begin to enter selection criteria to narrow down your audience, Facebook will provide the approximate number of people that your ad may reach. Keep in mind this is an estimate only and never exact. Depending on your outcome goals, budget size, and ideal target audience for each ad, you'll want to strike that ideal balance between having too broad or too narrow of an audience. There's no "right" set of numbers, but we'll provide some guidelines later in the chapter.

Let's examine the main selection criteria available when creating an ad.

Locations

Locations, also known as geo-targeting, are pretty straightforward. You can enter one or more of the following:

- Country
- State/Province
- City
- Zip Code

City targeting is not available in all countries, and zip codes only apply in the United States. At least one geographic selection is required when choosing an audience (in theory, all other criteria can be left blank). One nice feature is that you can select a mile radius for a given city to include nearby areas, such as "Chicago +10 miles." Also, you can use exclusion targeting to leave out specific locations within its larger geo-context, e.g., target all of California, but exclude Los Angeles and San Diego. Or start with a city like Los Angeles but exclude a select number of zip codes within to target a particular area.

Demographics

These filters target people based on age, gender, relationship status, profession, education, life events, and some social affiliations. The first level categories are listed below, with a couple of them expanded to show examples of next level choices (these aren't complete).

- Age range, from 13 - 64 (or don't specify)
- Gender
- Language
- Relationship
- Education
  - Education Level
  - Fields of study
  - Schools
- Work
  - Employer
  - Job Titles
  - Industries
- Politics
- Home
- Parents
- Life Events
  - New job
  - New relationship

- Newly engaged (3 months, 6 months, 1 year)
- Newlywed (3 months, 6 months, 1 year)
- Recently moved
- Upcoming birthday

Interests

These filters are based on people's expressed interests, hobbies, and pages they like on Facebook, as well as information based on ads they've clicked on, apps they use, content posted on their timelines, and keywords associated with pages they've liked. Facebook provides a broad list of categories to start, each of which can be drilled into further to reveal more defined interests. Top level category include:

- Business & Industry
- Entertainment
- Family & Relationships
- Fitness & Wellness
- Food & Drink
- Hobbies & Activities
- Shopping & Fashion
- Sports & Outdoors
- Technology

Some examples of next level categories include:

Hobbies & Activities
- Arts & music
- Current events
- Home & garden
- Pets
- Politics & social issues
- Travel
- Vehicles

Food & Drink
- Alcohol
- Beverages
- Cooking
- Cuisine
- Food
- Restaurants

Each next level category can be further drilled down to another target level. For example, under Alcohol, you will find beer, wine, and distilled beverages. Cuisine will have Italian, Chinese, Greek, Indian, etc. Pets will have dogs, cats, birds, fish, horses, and more. There are literally hundreds and hundreds of categories and segments to choose from.

Precise Interests

In addition to the list of categories that Facebook provides, you can type any keyword, term, phrase, interest, or existing business or fan page name and find millions of additional attributes and suggestions. For example, to drill further into the world of Italian cuisine (potential reach: 17.2 million in the US), we could type in "pasta" instead and see our reach drop to 4.2 million. Go even more specific with "spaghetti" and the audience narrows further to 920 thousand. Additionally, when you type in a keyword like spaghetti, Facebook will provide a list of related suggestions based on the data it has. As you can see in the picture, this includes SpaghettiOs (a brand), spaghetti with meatballs or spaghetti Bolognese (specific dishes), Spaghetti Warehouse (a restaurant) and even spaghetti strap (fashion) and spaghetti westerns (movies)!

Interests	Spaghetti		Browse
	Spaghetti		**4,264,614** people
Behaviors	SpaghettiOs	+	**Description:** People who have expressed an interest in or like pages related to *Spaghetti*
	Spaghetti with meatballs	+	
More Categories	**Spaghetti** Warehouse	+	
Connections	**Spaghetti** strap	+	
	spaghetti westerns	+	
	spaghetti bolognese	+	

As you can see, the options are almost endless, and you can combine as many interests as makes sense. And if Interests aren't enough, we next have Behaviors.

Behaviors

Behaviors are based on activities that people do on or off Facebook that reflect things like purchase behavior or intent, device usage, travel preferences, and more. Facebook works with trusted third-party partners Acixom, Datalogix, and Epsilon in a privacy-safe way to construct these behavior categories via transactional data, survey information, and other online and offline activity. User profiles are anonymously matched, and advertisers can never access personal information or target specific people. It's worth noting that some other categories within Demographics and Interests above are also sourced from these partners whenever data is not self-reported, such as income levels and home value among others. And, most of this data is available for the US only.

The top level Behavior categories include:

- Automotive
- Charitable donations
- Digital activities
- Financial
- Mobile Device User
- Purchase behavior
- Residential profiles
- Travel

The subcategories and drill-down capabilities within each behavior are extensive. For example, in Automotive, you can target new or used vehicle shoppers, owners of a particular make or style, purchase characteristics, and more. Charitable donations allow you to target specific areas like animal welfare, environmental, arts and cultural, political, religious, veterans, and world relief causes. Financial provides a variety of insurance, investment, and spending methods data to target, and as the name implies, Purchase Behavior allows you to drill deep into every conceivable category of products as well as buyer profiles, purchase habits, store types, and subscription services. And if you are a mobile app developer or have products and services related to the mobile or tablet space, this Mobile behavior category is an excellent way to hone in on this particular audience segment. Combine this with the option to only place your ads within Mobile News Feeds (excluding desktop users), and you have a one-two power punch that specifically targets the 80% of all Facebook users who access via mobile.

Connections

Finally, Facebook gives you advanced connection targeting options, whereby you can target only people who are connected to your page, app, or event (great for reaching out exclusively to your existing fan base); the ability to target *their* friends specifically; and the option to only target those NOT connected to you page, app, or event (great for expanding your audience, reaching new people, and not putting an existing offer in front of people who may have already purchased, attended, etc.).

Audience Definition Summary

To wrap this up with an example using a theme we started above, let's create a hypothetical case of a female food writer who is passionate about Italian cuisine, has an active foodie blog, and is getting ready to release a brand new cookbook in a couple months. Her goal is to generate some buzz and build her pre-launch email list of subscribers so that she can later promote her book to them. She has a sample collection of delicious recipes compiled as a free giveaway offer (her "lead magnet"), and wants to drive traffic to her website for sign-ups. Her best go-to recipe is an amazing vegetarian lasagna, and a major focus of her is book is on healthy, fresh, and nutritious versions of classic recipes. For her first ad, she has a mouth-watering photograph of a piping hot piece of lasagna beautifully presented, with enticing ad copy, and targeted to the following audience:

Audience Definition

Your audience is defined.

Specific — Broad

Audience Details:
- Location:
  - United States
- Age:
  - 25 - 55
- Gender:
  - female
- Interests:
  - Lasagne
- Behaviors:
  - Natural and organics or Healthy and fit

Potential Reach: 100,000 people

As you can see, Facebook provides a nice graphical representation of your audience size and selection. In this case, we have females between 25-55 years old who have already expressed interest in or have liked pages related to lasagna and who are buyers of natural and organic health food products, and whose activities strongly suggest they are healthy and fit. This reaches a nice audience size of around one hundred thousand people (between 50,000-100,000 is a good starting point to work with).

Will this be her best target audience? The only way to know is test it and ideally run multiple different ads to different segments. For example, she could separately target the "spaghetti" fans with a relevant photo, or with a different set of ad copy pursue busy working moms who are looking for "quick and delicious meals for the family on the go". For a broader audience, she could target people who like cooking, cooking shows, other recipe sites, or specific pages related to Italian food or culture.

Note: While beyond the scope of this chapter, running any successful advertising campaign is an iterative process that involves testing, measuring, optimizing, and re-testing all the different components (including your ad creative — title, body text, image, etc.) until you find the right combinations that produce the winning results you are after (whether it's clicks, likes, conversions, sales, downloads, etc.), while managing your budget appropriately, and ensuring a positive return on investment (ROI).

In summary, I hope you see the power and almost endless combination of locations, demographics, interests, and behaviors you can use to target and segment your ideal audience. Any discussion about reaching your perfect audience would not be complete without reviewing three other advanced targeting capabilities within Facebook. We'll cover them next.

Custom Audiences

As Facebook states, "Sometimes the most valuable audience is the one you already have a connection with." Custom Audiences lets you find your offline audiences and audiences existing elsewhere who are also on Facebook and use them as the target audience for your ads. You can upload your own customer list, email list, or base it on visitors to your website or users of your mobile app. You can create several different custom audiences and segment them in any way you choose, such as current customers, prospects, attendees to a webinar or event you held, different subsets of your email list, etc. There are many potential benefits and uses for this.

First, you could target people on your email list with a specific offer or announcement. Why would you do this if you can just email them directly? The reality is that less than 20% of emails get opened and read, so this is a great way to reach out and get your message in front of them that they may not see otherwise. It's also an excellent way to re-engage with them and drive them back to your website for a special offer or promotion, have them like your Facebook page, and to maintain top-of-mind presence. If you create a custom audience of active customers with recent purchases, you can offer them a loyalty program or limited time "thank you" discount to drive more sales. Another audience could be customers who haven't purchased in the last 12 months and you entice them back with a special "Welcome back" promotion. Or offer a special "new customer sale" to just your custom audience of prospects who haven't purchased yet.

Custom audiences are also an excellent way to *exclude* existing customers or subscribers from seeing your ad. This is perfect when trying to only target new customers or grow your email list with new subscribers, so that you are not wasting money putting your ad in front of people who are already on your list. Additionally, you can apply all the targeting options previously discussed to narrow your custom audience further, such as by location or interest.

Finally, please note that Facebook has very specific terms and conditions that you must review and accept before creating your first custom audience. Always (always!) play by the rules and never violate their terms of service (e.g., You can't upload purchased lists, "scraped" Facebook IDs, target individual users, etc.), or else you risk getting your account banned. Many people have learned this the hard way; don't let this be you!

Lookalike Audiences

Imagine the ability to reach new people who are likely interested in your business because they have similar traits (based on location, interests, and demographics) to customers you already have! Or imagine expanding your reach to similar people who have already liked your Facebook page, or have visited your website.

Lookalike audiences do just that. You can target individuals with similar traits as one of your existing custom audiences or for your page or website. It's a great way to take a smaller audience and greatly expand your reach to those already with an affinity for what you have to offer.

Facebook gives you the option to either optimize for similarity (targeting the top 1%) which will be smaller but more precise, or optimize for reach (top 5%) that will be less precise but reach greater numbers. Lookalike audiences can only target one country at a time, but you can create new lists for as many countries as needed. As with Custom audiences, you can apply additional targeting to further narrow down as needed, use exclusion targeting, and even target multiple lookalike audiences for a single ad.

Website Custom Audiences (WCA) & Retargeting

A relatively recent feature known as Website Custom Audiences lets you target people who visit your website or even specific pages on your website. This is a very powerful capability with enormous potential, allowing you to custom tailor an ad specifically based on the content or pages that they've viewed. There are many possible ways to utilize this, including: reach people who have visited your website or blog, but haven't become a fan of your page or subscriber yet (your ad asks them to like or subscribe); reach people who have visited your site within a particular time window (last 30-180 days) so you can promote new content or blog posts that drive traffic back to your website; even more powerful, with advanced logic you can target only those visitors who *haven't* seen your latest blog post yet by excluding those who already have!

Here are some more examples. If you have an ecommerce store or another site with content, products, or services organized in various categories, imagine being able to tailor an ad that's relevant only to visitors of a particular category. Or imagine having a landing page with a newsletter sign-up or giveaway offer, or a sales page for a particular product. You can create one website custom audience for those who visited the landing page or sales page; a second one for those who reached the "Thank You" page or "Order Completed" page; and then run an ad that targets the former and excludes the latter, which will identify everyone who visited the landing or sales page but *didn't* opt-in or buy. You can then re-target them with an ad that invites them to come back, or offer an additional bonus for download or a special one-time discount if they complete the purchase. You can even run an ad that surveys your audience and ask them why they abandoned the cart (perhaps they just got distracted and forgot, and now your "magical" ad appeared and prompted them to return and buy). The possibilities are truly endless!

The best part about these website custom audiences is that they are dynamic, meaning the audience will continue to grow as visitors come to your site over time. To enable this, all you need is a custom audience pixel (a small snippet of code) installed once on your website and Facebook will start building this list automatically from that point forward. You can also install conversion tracking pixels to monitor specific actions that will be reported back to Facebook's Ads Manager tool for tracking and reporting purposes. This is an excellent way to measure the true ROI of a campaign based on cost per conversion, where "conversion" could be any action that you want to monitor — checkouts, new registrations, leads, page views, etc.

As you can see, these more advanced targeting capabilities are truly powerful and we've just scratched the surface on what's possible. As Facebook continues to build out its advertising platform and evolve its capabilities and tools, you as a business owner (and now advertiser!) will only continue to benefit from these improvements to reach your objectives through the power of Facebook marketing.

Summary

In summary, I hope we achieved our objectives and adequately conveyed why it pays to advertise, why Facebook is one of the best advertising platforms to use, and why Facebook's audience selection capabilities are unmatched in their scope, breadth, and depth of targeting. At the same time, I hope you got excited about the possibilities this presents for your business! Facebook truly provides the means to getting in front of your right audience and find the people who will love your business.

There is one final statistic to leave you with. Facebook recently announced they have more than 30 million active small & medium business (SMB) pages and over 1.5 million active advertisers. This is both good news and a call to action. If your business currently isn't on Facebook yet or has been in a dormant or "ignored" state for some time, start now or start fresh again with a renewed sense of purpose and excitement! There's no better time to leverage Facebook's platform to grow your business. And with a relatively small ratio between total business pages and those who currently advertise, this is a prime opportunity to position yourself ahead of your competition and reach your market more quickly and effectively.

As mentioned earlier, audience selection and targeting is only one component of running a successful Facebook campaign. Additional considerations include ad design and content, ad formats, managing the budget and bidding strategy, testing, optimization, tracking and monitoring results, and ROI. This list isn't intended to overwhelm or scare you from taking action. On the contrary, we encourage you to jump in and start exploring! Check out the extensive help pages and business sections on Facebook where you'll find a wealth of information available to help you get started. Finally, know that you can run a campaign for as little as $5 per day, so there's no reason not to give it a try!

To assist you with this process, we've prepared some free resources to download as a bonus for readers of this chapter and book. They can be yours by visiting
http://www.wowcreativemedia.com/MoneyBookBonus

Additionally, if we can be of any assistance with your Facebook advertising needs or support your other online marketing efforts, we offer consulting, done-with-you coaching and full done-for-you services in a variety of areas. Please visit http://www.wowcreativemedia.com to review our services and schedule a free consultation.

About the Author

Dave Pittman is founder, principal consultant and Chief Wowpreneur at Wow Creative Media, LLC, an online marketing, new media, and business growth consulting company that helps business owners, entrepreneurs, and professionals build their online presence and platform, simplify and automate their marketing, and grow their business. He loves delivering Wow results and a Wow experience for his clients, and helps them discover and unleash their own Wow to promote and accelerate their business and profits.

With over 21 years' experience in the high tech industry ranging from small startups to global Fortune 100 companies, Dave's breadth of experiences include: consultant, analyst, database architect, web designer and developer, project manager, and marketing intelligence leader of global teams delivering multi-million dollar initiatives. Now, Dave takes his passion for marketing and technology and helps people and businesses leverage these to their strategic advantage for greater benefit, enjoyment, productivity, and profit. He is an Author Expert Marketing Machines Certified Consultant, a comprehensive framework that helps people build their online presence and platform from which they can position, publish, productize, promote, and profit from their knowledge, experience and expertise, and become a recognized authority in their field.

How To Be a Highly Paid Speaker, Trainer, or Coach
by Cydney O'Sullivan

I have owned businesses for over 30 years, and I genuinely believe that thanks to modern technologies, the most amazing marketing tools for your business today are Speaking and Workshops. As a professional marketer, I help my clients use almost every tool you could think of to promote their businesses, but the fastest way to create connection and add a heap of income to your business is to get out and meet your customers, prospects, and leads. Get out there and network, show them how much you care about them, offer them your products and programs, and watch your business grow. When done right, it's magic and it's fun!

I'm going to share with you how to use your knowledge and life experience for positioning so that your ideal clients start seeking YOU out, and FINDING you.

I'm going to blast through the success formula that my partner and I have been teaching our high paying clients to help them get clarity and business success, and what we've seen work over and over in a variety of industries. I'll share what's helped us generate over $14 million dollars in new sales over the last four years, when everyone else was telling us there was a recession.

Would you agree that writing a professional book full of great advice that showcases you as an expert in your field will help establish you as a more credible and authoritative choice over your competition who hasn't?

Did you know that writing a short ebook can give you fantastic clarity about your expertise and help share it with others? **The secret is that when you back such a book up with a great website, strong social and traditional media presence, and public speaking, it's an absolutely winning combination**

for success. We have assisted many experts to use this combination to make hundreds of thousands and even millions of dollars.

The Formula to Experts Success™ – The Four P's

The formula is made up of four components and it's important to get them in the right order. Implementing them in the wrong order often leads to a massive waste of time, effort, and lots of wasted money.

They are:

1. **Positioning**
2. **Packaging**
3. **Promotion**
4. **Processes**

Once you know how to fill an event with the right audience, make an attractive offer that is of genuine value to some of the people in the audience, process your orders efficiently, and then deliver on your sales promises, you can literally earn tens of thousands to millions of dollars per event.

If you don't want to run your own events, but wish to become an accomplished speaker who is able to create demand and close sales, you can make an equally impressive fortune speaking at other people's events, seminars, webinars, teleseminars, certification programs, and trainings. That's just a few of the places that you can find opportunities to practice sales presentations. There are also Chambers of Commerce,

Community Centers, Libraries, Networking events—you're only limited by your own ability to grow.

The Foundational Pillars of The Experts Success™ Formula

Positioning

In the speaking and training business, positioning yourself for success is an absolute game changer.

1. To position yourself effectively as a leader in your area of expertise, you should research your market and take the time to know your customers' needs, pains, and pleasure points.
2. Understand the importance of and make the investment in developing a professional brand, bio, and marketing message.
3. Seek out and invest in relationships with influencers and your marketplace and create alliances to leverage your credibility and open doors faster.

Packaging

Once you are clear on your positioning, THAT is when successful businesses develop Packaging

1. Craft and practice your unique script to engage audiences and separate yourself from the competition.
2. Create offers and products specifically tailored to your ideal market; they should feel highly valuable, irresistible, and desirable.
3. Invest in marketing funnels that lead your audiences to offers that are relevant.

Promotions

We see so many businesses pouring money into paid promotions when they don't even have their positioning and marketing funnels in place. This can drain your finances, distract your focus, and ultimately hurt your business.

1. Set up authoritative web presences to collect prospect contact information so you can build relationships and referral communities.
2. Use marketing and media to get access to major distribution networks.
3. Use cutting-edge technologies like social media marketing, video marketing, and webinars for greater reach and competitive edge.

All the while developing your automated systems...

Processes

This is an area we rarely see businesses getting right.

1. Successful businesses have simple systems that control the client experience from the first sales contact through

to a paid product or service, and even the after-sales experiences.
2. Have simple sales processes that make it easy to take prospects to clients.
3. Maximize the results of their marketing efforts and collect the revenues in the most automated and leveraged way possible, always reviewing and improving on their systems and customer experience.

Thanks to modern technologies, even very small businesses can have professional processes now that allow them to process large orders and high volumes of sales. It's not unusual for well-organized speakers today to process hundreds of thousands of dollars in orders at a single event. They can make the annual revenue of most small- to medium-sized businesses in a few hours!

1. Choose Your Leadership Position

Choose your niche and topic of expertise

Your qualifications, life experience, or passionate interests will largely determine what particular niche you choose to plant your stake in and call your own. But, if you're smart, you'll also take into consideration market demand, how 'cashed up' a market sector is, and the competition.

Also research your local market and global market to find out who you are competing with in that category.

Keep it Simple!!

Don't overcomplicate this process. This is where we see most inexperienced people wasting effort, time, and money—making things much more complicated than they need to be.

Is there another person doing a great job with their positioning you could model? Who do you think their target market is and how are they talking the language of that customer base?

2. Create a Game Plan

At this stage, you need a game plan that shows you understand your market. You've worked out the numbers, worked out the best marketing strategies, and delivery options so you can know when you'll hit your revenue targets. If you don't hit your targets, you'll be able to adjust the plan and know where you went wrong and correct the plan. Then you can leverage your sales and marketing funnels to allow you growth.

Shortcuts

Once you're executing your plan, there are plenty of shortcuts—outsourcing, modeling, and technology. These are advanced topics and we could write a book on each of these! Don't let these be distractions and delay your forward momentum.

If you hire others to help where you are inexperienced or to manage areas that are not your strength, it should pay off in speed to market. But be careful, finding genuine support in this industry is a bit of a minefield. Check out any service providers and support teams extensively. Do your due diligence.

3. Write The Presentation To Get Clear On The Message

Now it's time to write your presentation. Here is what we advise most strongly:

- Create Your Presentation
- Test it with small audiences (webinar or small group of friends) before going live; practice, tweak and present again
- Test present again to a small, friendly live audience and incorporate valid and qualified feedback
- Test your presentation on another audience and incorporate valid and qualified feedback
- Practice, practice, practice

What Makes a Good Speech—Crafting the Presentation

There are as many ways to give a speech as there are topics, audiences, and different kinds of people in the world. There are inspirational speeches, entertaining presentations, keynotes, educational, and sales presentations, to name just a few of the different styles.

For the purposes of this chapter, I'll focus on a combination of styles that is designed to engage the interest of the audience, invoke an emotional connection, and create a desire in as many as possible that leads to them deciding to move forward with you in some way towards a commercial outcome.

Your speech should be entertaining, engaging, inspiring, authentic, and paced so that your audience come on a journey with you. There are a number of well-established techniques that you can incorporate into your presentation that encourage your audience to interact with and feel more connected and trusting towards you. These can be learned in our advanced trainings, and they are very powerful.

4. Establishing Your Expertise

Once you have your presentation and are clear on the area of expertise where you are going out to market, it's time to start building up your expert credibility.

Here are some ways to get started:
- Social proof—any awards, special achievements, client endorsements, well-known companies you've worked for or with, big name clients who don't mind you using their names on your websites and brochures
- Case studies—showcase your successes and those of your clients
- Testimonials—ask high-profile people you've worked with to give you an endorsement or testimonial in writing, audio, or video form. If you have audio or video, it's easy to transcribe to written. Also get testimonials from your clients and customers. Think creatively; for instance, even your suppliers might like to give you testimonials.
- Media and Published Credibility—if you've had any books or articles published, been featured in the newspaper, on the radio, or on TV, consider adding these to your website and marketing.
- Speaking Engagements—if you've spoken with other big name speakers, or if you've spoken at big events. These can also be mentioned in your marketing collateral.

Marketing Online

Marketing online has become one of the most cost-effective and results-effective ways to launch a business quickly and profitably in today's market.

- Build a professional business site that showcases your business and speaking programs that is search engine optimized to the terms people would use to find you as a solution provider or speaker in your niche.
- Use Social Media platforms to appear professional; in particular LinkedIn, Facebook, Google+, Instagram, Twitter, and Pinterest.

Don't Be Cheap on Your Way to Success!
Remember! Don't be cheap on your branding and websites

Professionals want to work with other professionals and they WILL check you out and they will judge you on ugly, outdated, or cheap looking websites and marketing materials. Invest in your professional image.

5. Packages

What should you sell as a professional speaker?

Firstly, make sure you like delivering what you're selling and want to talk about it and help people on an ongoing basis.

Other People's Products and Services, Training, or Programs

Where most people first get into giving public presentations is either as an educator or trainer, or selling for others as part of their job, or often people find out they are a good speaker while promoting network marketing programs.

You Might Prefer to Sell Your Own Programs, Coaching and Trainings

We recommend that once you know your niche and topic, you write books about it and that will give you the foundation to create training programs, coaching programs, and certification trainings and programs. Or you might prefer to create your consulting, coaching, or training program and produce books later, or never at all.

Tips:

- Create your packages in a way that makes it very easy for people to buy
- Make them relevant, market appropriate, and competitive

6. Marketing Funnels—The Magic Formula to Acquire and Nurture Leads

Marketing Funnels are magic once effectively planned, built, and set in place. This is one of the most important aspects of the success formula, and one of the areas we see most commonly left out or poorly executed. Not setting up

marketing funnels is literally leaving most of the cash in your business completely and inexcusably untapped.

The goal of the nurturing process is to convert the leads who show initial interest into prospects, then through a natural filtering process, convert them into customers and raving fans.

7. Set Up Your Delivery Process and Systems

Make sure whatever you sell—you can deliver!

You need to be able to deliver what you market. Few things will hurt your business more than getting your positioning right, your packaging right, your sales working, and then failing to deliver on your promise.

Automation and technology

We recommend products and services that can be delivered digitally with all of today's modern technologies. Though with the amazing online retail facilities that are available, it's not hard to deliver physical books and programs through Amazon, eBay, and other similar online platforms that have massive audiences and distribution networks in place already.

8. Promotion

Effective Marketing

We recommend you focus on marketing that monetizes along the way. Whether it's starting with free marketing options and seeing what works, or paid advertising—there will be some mediums and strategies that are more effective than others, depending on your topic, niche, offer, and target markets.

Getting your marketing right can make the difference between getting in front of five people a month and 5000 people a month, and making lots of sales or pouring money down the drain with a fire hose-sized tap. With today's technologies, **our clients regularly make $50,000 to a $100,000 dollars** from a simple, but strategic, marketing campaign.

If your marketing is not producing **revenue**, it's almost certainly the wrong marketing.

Get help from experienced results-focused professionals with a track record of success.

Webinars and Teleseminars

Webcasts and telecasts, also known as webinars and teleseminars, are a brilliant and now easily accessible technology to do trainings and speeches from online to an audience anywhere in the world. We have done webinars with attendees from all over the world at once! Depending on the platform you choose, you can accommodate an audience of one to thousands. And the cost per broadcast will most likely vary by such factors as number of attendees, though there are now plenty of free options for broadcasting over the internet.

Social Media

Most people have social media accounts now, such as Facebook and LinkedIn, so a great place to start building up a supportive community for your events, speaking engagements, and campaigns is by connecting with social media.

Social media promotional campaigns can be very effective, but do take some time to set up properly. We recommend that this tends to be more of an advanced strategy, unless you are a great networker and already have a large following of your target market to promote to.

Emails

Having an effective emailing system in place and crafting engaging emails should be part of your promotional strategy. Then focus on building up your subscriber list every time you go out and speak or network.

9. Sales

Selling

Influence is what closes the sale, and it's what helps our customers find us, trust us, and enables us to improve their lives. We all use it on some level. We just have to get over all the negative hype associated with the word 'sales' or—on an even deeper level—the baggage associated with asking for money.

If you are not selling your services or products, then you are not serving the world with your true gifts. You are cheapening your brand and hurting the industry in which you should be a proud leader and specialist. If you aren't joyfully selling in your business, we'd like to help you get over whatever is holding you back—quickly and seriously. Because you are here reading this book about being ready to launch and if you don't get this one thing sorted, all the hard work you put in will come to a bottleneck and hold back your success!

Follow-up: *Do you want $1 million or will you stop at $100,000?*

The secret is in the follow up. It's so important, and staying in touch can be automated using a well-designed sales funnel. With the technology we have today, there is no reason that you cannot do this quite easily and it usually makes a huge financial improvement for the business.

There are great emotional and financial rewards for those who succeed in this industry; wealth, freedom, recognition, and the joy of being able to facilitate the ongoing transformation of yourself and others. Sharing your gifts for financial and spiritual wealth, and being able to help those less fortunate, are only some of the rewards of success.

Where you can find us:

We have so much more to teach you! Please visit our website http://ExpertsSuccess.com.au/ for your free in-depth step-by-step guide to speaking success and join our community. We regularly hold value-packed online trainings, and live workshops across Australia, Las Vegas and other US cities.

To Your Great and Fabulous Success!!

About the Author

Cydney O'Sullivan has been a business 'turn around' expert most of her career. In her years as a business, real estate, and stock market investor, she has made millions, as well as some costly mistakes. She now enjoys assisting others achieve their own success as authors and speakers through her business ExpertsSuccess.com.

She is a 9 times best-selling business author sharing her own experiences of turning value and service into profit.

Her business advice has been featured in national newspapers and magazines, and in many books. She is the founder of several training programs including Experts Success™, Millionaires Academy™, Best Seller Success™, Expert Success Summit™ and Social Superstar Secrets™. Website: http://ExpertsSuccess.com.au

Become an Instant Authority with the Power of Publishing
by Everett O'Keefe

I was on a jet a couple weeks ago flying home from Virginia after working there with one of my clients. Seated next me was a clearly affluent gentleman, dressed in casual but expensive clothes. When I asked him what he did for a living, he shared how he had sold a prosperous business that was a landmark in his community, and he retired afterward, content to enjoy the fruits of his labor. When he asked what I did, I told him I am an Amazon #1 Bestselling Author and that I work with business owners and professionals to position them as experts, through authorship among other things. He stopped and did a double take.

"I don't think I have ever met an author before," he said.

The truth is, most people are just like him. They have never met someone who has published a book. And when they do meet an author, they are immediately both surprised and impressed. Now I could have told him I own a marketing company. He has met plenty of people who own marketing companies. But until he met me, this affluent, well-connected business owner had not ever met an author.

Authors are a rare breed. Though many people would like to write a book, very few ever even start a book, and far fewer finish and publish one. This is strange when you consider that it is easier than ever to create and launch a book. The tools and services available to us now make it a far simpler and more accessible process than in previous years.

Until recently, prospective authors had to go it the traditional way by either securing a book deal from a publisher or by spending a lot of money to self-publish. The challenge of getting a publishing deal is that the large publishing houses are publishing fewer and fewer books, choosing to stand behind only established personalities and authors. The chance that you will get a book proposal accepted by a publishing house is almost nil. And self-publishing has historically been an expensive affair. For you to be an author, you would usually have to make a significant investment just to get your book made, and then you had to buy a large stock of books. Poke around the garages of people who self-published before 2005 and you will likely find cases (if not pallets) of books. And these authors find themselves loaded down with books they are unable to easily sell or distribute.

But all this has changed. With the advent of print-on-demand or "POD" technology, it is now possible for nearly anyone to become an author. There is no longer the need to have pallets or cases of books printed. Instead, many sources can print your book one copy at a time, only when it is needed. This is liberating because it significantly lowers the financial threshold of authorship. The hard costs associated with self-publishing have almost disappeared!

And yet, very few people know this! The average person thinks that creating and publishing a book are as hard as ever. This is a huge advantage to you, because it is easier and cheaper than ever to *become* an author, but the impact of *being* an author hasn't lessened at all!

Take a look at a quote from author Seth Godin:

"The return on equity and return on time for authors and for publishers is horrendous. If you're doing it for the money, you're going to be disappointed. On the other hand, a book gives you leverage to spread an idea and a brand far and wide. There's a worldview that's quite common that says that people who write books know what they are talking about and that a book confers some sort of authority.[1]

---

[1] http://sethgodin.typepad.com/seths_blog/2005/07/advise_for_auth.html

On the one hand, Godin is correct. Those who write a book to make money *on* the book itself are in for a letdown. Even famous and well-capitalized authors make very little money on a book itself. Royalties are very low, and the expense and effort it takes to market and promote a book are extreme. He is also correct about the sense of authority granted to authors. People see authors as an elite and gifted class. If you have a book, you are assumed to be an expert on your subject, almost regardless of the content of your book. Really, creating a book, whether you sell one copy or not, makes you an instant authority on your subject.

Fortunately, Mr. Godin is wrong about the first point he makes. The return on investment is *not* "horrendous." *If* you create and publish your book in the correct way and then properly leverage the book, it can be very profitable. Let me explain.

When I wrote the Amazon #1 Bestseller, *The Video Tractor Beam: Dominate Your Field and Attract New Clients and Customers with Online Video*, some amazing things happened. First, I made very little money from the book launch. The "rush the charts" strategy we employed for the launch was very successful in gaining a bestseller ranking, and that was the goal of the launch. But we made very little in the way of royalties. That's fine. That was part of the plan. Second, I made a substantial profit from the *effect* of the book. I had people who never knew anything about what I do suddenly contact me to help them with video creation and video marketing. I had people coming up to me and commenting about my book and success. My co-author, John Riding, had an acquaintance approach him at McDonalds one day and say, "So are you some sort of big deal now?" He had met John one time at church and knew nothing else about John other than the fact that he had recently launched a book that had become a bestseller on Amazon.

There's Money in This Book

While we made very little in the way of royalties on the book, it helped catapult our business because of the extra weight and authority it granted to us and because of the expert status it conferred.

But can I let you in on a secret? The truth of the matter is that we didn't write the book to be seen as authorities in video creation and video marketing. Although the book absolutely accomplished this goal, we wrote it simply as a "proof of concept." We created the book only to test a new book creation and launch strategy. We knew that creating and launching books was something we wanted to help people accomplish, and we wanted to use ourselves as guinea pigs to test the methods and perfect the process. I am so glad we did. This "proof of concept" book not only allowed us to test our methods (and get some mistakes out of the way), but it also made us an instant authority in the video creation and marketing field. In retrospect, we should have written the book on the subject of book creation and publishing! But that is okay.

Since launching our own book and watching it become a #1 bestseller on Amazon, we have had seven consecutive successful launches of our client's books (and a music album!). Several of these have been #1 bestsellers on Amazon, and all have been in the top ten. Incidentally, the album we launched, *We Are Your Church* by Celebration Worship, reached the top 50 of *all* albums on Amazon and top 60 of all albums on iTunes in addition to getting #1 and #2 positions in Contemporary Christian music categories respectively. It even made the *Billboard* magazine charts!

All of these projects have been successful in elevating their authors and their brands. In fact, one of our clients, Frank Leyes, has seen his speaking income increase 600% since launching his bestseller, *The Way of Wealth: 7 Steps To Financial Freedom In A World Of Economic Dependence*. I don't share this with you to brag about what we do for our clients, but to show you the impact of being an author and especially of being a bestselling author. While Seth Godin is correct that you shouldn't expect to make money *on* a book, you *should* expect to make money *with* a book.

And there are lots of ways to leverage a book. Here are a few:

The 100-page flyer

Print-on-demand books can be cheap. Very cheap. Most of the books we have launched or published for clients can be purchased by the author for under $3 a book, in quantities as low as *one*! At a few dollars a book, you can afford to use this book as a 100-page flyer. So rather than leaving behind that single-page, glossy thing you had printed at Kinko's or a printer, leave a copy of your book with prospective clients. Your "stock in trade" will immediately skyrocket. And trust me—your competition is not doing this. In fact, do this and you will have no competition.

The thick business card

When someone asks you for a business card, give them a book. Seriously. And then watch the expression on that person's face. He or she will be shocked and probably tell you that s/he has never been handed a book instead of a business card. If you want, go the extra mile and sign the book too! Heck, you are an author. You might as well ham it up a bit!

The perfect gift

When meeting with prospects, give them a copy of your book as a gift. Your prospect will almost always feel grateful...for several reasons. First, almost nobody has been given a book by the author of that book. It is a unique experience. Second, a book has a high perceived value. Though you know it is really just a hundred (or whatever) pages of ink and paper, your prospect sees the price on the back cover. Of course, he or she knows you didn't pay the retail price, but you can bet your prospect has no idea it only cost you a few dollars. Third, a book has "thud value." We are talking about the sound it makes when you place it on someone's desk or coffee table. It has weight and body to it, which increases the perceived value.

The back-of-room sale

If you speak or hold workshops, sell your book! After you speak, many people will want more of you. What better way than to send them home with a book, especially if they pay for it. This is one way you can actually make a limited amount of money on the book itself. Naturally, you will look more like the expert if you are not the one doing the selling. Try to get someone else to staff the back table. If that is not possible and you trust your audience, use an honor system. Put a sign next to a stack of books with some sort of money receptacle so people can drop money in the box and take a book. We have found several attractive locking suggestion boxes on Amazon that work really well for this.

Office décor

Display your book at work, in your office and in the waiting room or lobby if you have one. Pick up a plate holder from the craft store or Target and use this to display "your baby" in a professional manner. Place a copy on your desk or bookshelf where visiting clients and associates can see it. Place another in the lobby somewhere. For a really nice touch, get a copy of your book framed and place it on the wall like a plaque.

Writing and launching a book is a big accomplishment, and people should know about it. And nobody will consider you to be ostentatious if you display your creation.

Who needs magazines?

Instead of outdated magazines or big coffee table books, place a copy of your book in the reception area where people can read it. While clients or prospects are sitting and waiting for you, they will undoubtable pick up your book and thumb through it. Heck, make sure to let them sit out there for a few minutes to encourage this! By the time they meet with you, they will already consider you to be an expert in your field. And the book may have already planted some pain points (and your solutions) in their minds.

Get speaking gigs

Your ability to acquire a speaking gig is greatly increased when you are an author. Become a bestselling author and your attractiveness as a speaker is multiplied. Event organizers are always looking for effective speakers. But they are also frequently concerned about how attendees will perceive the list of speakers. Nobody wants to hire a "nobody." With a book under your belt, you are a celebrity, even if no one has heard of you. And the bestseller moniker makes you a certified celebrity of sorts. So when you introduce yourself to an event organizer of a speakers' bureau, start with "I am the author of...."

Let people know about your book

It is great being an author. It is even better when people know about it. Include your new accomplishment in your stationery, your email signature, your business card, and any other place it would be both beneficial and appropriate. People will not see this as bragging. They understand what a big deal it is to become an author (even if they don't know how easy it really is) and they will be impressed with your accomplishment.

Your Elevator Speech

Add your book to your elevator speech or 60-second commercial. When people ask you what you do, *start* with "I am the author of the Amazon bestselling book...." People will be very surprised. And they will ask you about it. The worst thing you can have happen after you give an elevator speech is for someone to say "oh, okay" and not ask any questions. Tell them you are an author, and they will ask questions about you, your book, and your expertise!

Do a press release

Send out a press release about your book. There are some great services available to prepare and distribute a press release, and many will deliver your press release to thousands of news outlets and track the placement of the release. This is critical. Get a report from the service showing where your press release has been picked up. Then leverage this! If your press release was featured by a Fox or ABC affiliate, use that in your marketing. Technically, you and your book have now been featured by that news outlet. They chose to publish your press release because they (or their software systems) determined it to be newsworthy. So don't be afraid to say "as featured on ABC" if ABC has chosen to feature you and your book in this fashion.

There isn't the space available in this chapter to tell you how to become an author. But I *can* tell you that it is easier than ever and faster than ever. You can make it all happen in under 30 days if you are motivated. *The Video Tractor Beam* went from our heads, to print, to #1 Small Business Marketing book at Amazon in under 30 days!

The hardest part is writing the book...so don't write it. Seriously. Instead, sit down and make some bullet points that will help you organize your subject matter. If needed, reorder them. Then flesh each one out so you have enough detail to discuss each chapter. Then do that...on video or audio! That is the secret. Record yourself speaking the content of the book. Then get it transcribed. In this way, you can have your first draft completed in days rather than weeks or months. And don't worry about perfection. You can clean it up in subsequent drafts!

Then get your book edited and designed. Services like Elance are full of good editors who will edit and design your book for cheap. Find one and get it done.

Cover? You can use a number of online tools if you like, or seek an artist on Elance or Fivrr. Pay special attention to your cover. It is more important than any other part of your book. Many people will never open your book, so you need to make the cover really rock. Or sing. Either way, it needs to be an effective presentation of you and your brand.

Now your book is complete! And if you have gotten this far, you have surpassed more than 90% of budding authors, most of whom never complete a manuscript, let alone publish one. Lots of people talk about writing a book, and many actually start. ***Very few*** ever finish.

I need a couple more chapters to give you everything you need to know about publishing and launching your book. It is easier and faster than ever, but there are right and wrong ways to do this. And executing a bestseller launch on Amazon is lots of fun...but also tricky. Too little information can be dangerous. So rather than not give you enough information here, I have created a special resource just for readers of this book. It is a book creation, publishing and launching *mindmap* that I think you will find useful. It will show you the best practices you can use to create and launch your book. These are the same practices we have used for multiple Amazon #1 Bestseller launches, so we know they work.

However you decide to write and publish your book, *leverage it properly* to build your business and brand! There are few things more powerful than a book, and there are few titles more revered than "author" or "bestselling author." I look forward to the day I see *your* book on the Amazon charts!

Receive Everett's Publishing MindMap instantly! Just send an email to PublishingMindMap@The SolutionMachine.com. Yes, the email address is long, but the delivery of the mind map will be instant! And you can use it navigate this *incredibly rewarding* journey!

About the Author

Everett O'Keefe is the co-author of the Amazon #1 Bestseller *The Video Tractor Beam: Dominate Your Field and Attract New Clients and Customers with Online Video*. He and his business partner, John Riding, founded The Solution Machine, a cross-channel marketing company focusing on creating new experts and assisting experienced experts with product creation and back-end systems. Everett is certified in a wide variety of marketing strategies and tools, and these tools are "force multipliers" for him and his clients. As of this writing, Everett has helped create and/or launch a total of 8 Amazon bestsellers for his clients, including the 2013 debut of *The Way of Wealth* by Frank Leyes, which reached #1 Bestseller at Amazon in the highly competitive category of Money Management, besting books by Suze Orman, Dave Ramsey, and Clark Howard. His book and CD launches include 5 Amazon #1 bestsellers for his clients. Everett and his team continue to perform video production, product creation, and launches while allowing their clients to focus on their own areas of unique giftedness. He can be contacted at www.TheSolutionMachine.com or info@TheSolutionMachine.com.

Moving Up the Food Chain: Closing Bigger Internet Marketing Clients
by Joe (JT) Ippolito

For many years, I focused on helping local businesses get more traffic to their websites to help them grow their brick-and-mortar business, as well as their online business. It's a great feeling to see struggling entrepreneurs get back on track and become successful based on the things I taught them, such as how to use social media, Internet marketing, blogging, and mobile apps.

I would always show them how to use these techniques, and I would have people say that I'm teaching myself out of a client. But the reality is, while I felt good about making sure my clients could always be independent of my services, most of them didn't have the time or the desire to implement what I taught them; so I had a steady income anyway. As for those who wanted to try doing some of it themselves, they still always had me as a backup plan. It was a win-win situation.

I connected with these clients by advertising on Craigslist, networking at local events, and by word of mouth. Once you have a happy client, they not only continue to want your help, they also recommend you to their friends and family and anyone who also needs to grow their business.

It was easy to "close" these smaller clients. They were local and our first meetings were often in person. Once they saw what I did for others, they were begging me to help them! After that, we had in-person meetings from time to time, but most meetings were via email or on the phone, so I could work on the computer to make it all happen for them.

While I stayed busy doing online marketing and traffic-building for these wonderful appreciative people, their budgets were low. Understanding how hard the economy has hit so many people and businesses, I charged much less for my services than I probably should have. But helping people save their businesses, and literally changing people's lives as a result, has always been very satisfying to me.

And yet? One day someone pointed out that my techniques and strategies would work for big businesses as well. "Big businesses?" I asked. I always thought big companies had in-house Internet marketing teams and/or hired big fancy well-known specialists in the field. "Why would one of them want to hire a small entrepreneur like me to help them out?"

"Are you kidding?" my friend responded. "Have you seen how screwed-up some of their social media campaigns are? And how some of the companies are even losing money this quarter? Lots of people claim to be successful Internet marketers; but you have a great track record! Maybe if you start at a lower introductory price at the beginning (double what you get from the little local businesses), they'll take a chance on you and try out your services!"

That one conversation changed my life. It worked! I began to move up the food chain and started closing bigger and bigger clients. My income quickly tripled doing the same amount of work as I had been doing all along, and with the same fantastic results for my clients.

Do I continue to teach my clients everything and make them independent? Yes. Absolutely. Regardless of the size of the client company, I still provide personalized step-by-step procedures with their login information; and they still prefer that I do it all FOR them. But they appreciate my honesty and integrity. There is a lot of that missing in this business and they know it. Honesty, integrity, fair prices, and results combine to make the perfect combination for success.

But what about the local companies I had been helping? I hired a couple of freelancers who could still pitch in and ghostwrite blogs and social media posts; and I keep an eye on the situation because I genuinely care about the small local businesses who still need and trust me. What the larger companies with their big budgets provide for me is an amazing steady six-figure income per year.

Learning to delegate some tasks, and sticking with the strategies that work, have made this an awesome win-win situation for everyone. That's the way life and business should be. Genuinely care about each other and unselfishly help each other; because when you approach life and business from that perspective, great and wonderful things (including lots of money!) will flow into your life, seemingly easily and effortlessly because you're doing what you love to do.

While telling my story, you've learned some techniques for finding local clients and building your business by helping them build theirs. Would you like to learn some ways to move on up the food chain and land those big lucrative clients? Okay. Here we go!

Where to Find the Big Clients

REMEMBER: "Big Clients" aren't necessarily Fortune 500 companies. These are simply the ones who have the bigger budgets and the bigger needs.

1. **Target Your Market.** Don't just do a mass emailing. Do an online search and locate the type of company you'd like to work with. They can be located anywhere in the country. Then check out their website, media page, annual report, and social media. Get to know a few companies at a time and approach them with a personal touch, offering ideas and solutions and services tailored just for them.

2. **Regional Marketing Events.** You could even consider hosting or joint-sponsoring a half-day workshop. Regardless, go there and network.

3. **Big Digital and E-Commerce Events**, such as SES, AdTech, EComm Expo. Google the regional and national events in your field of expertise and make a working vacation out of it!

4. **Social Networking Channels.** Use the search engines of Facebook, Twitter, Google+, and LinkedIn to find companies you might be interested in being involved with. Get their attention by mentioning them in a tweet explaining how much you'd love to team up with their company. Connect through a LinkedIn group, etc.

5. **Blogs.** Find out which companies are blogging, and how well they're doing at it. That way, you can help them improve or at least give them a compliment. Also check out the best blogs in your field by typing in blog:keyword (use your own keyword!) in Google.

6. **Referrals.** Referrals from happy clients. Even small business clients know big business clients.

7. **Social Events.** Go to your high school and/or college reunion. Go to local events as well as regional and national ones. Attend fundraising events that attract an upscale crowd. You never know who you might meet. And if you only get one great contact, it will have been worth it. Keep in mind that the great contact might not be your next client, but might know someone who COULD be! The worst that could happen is that you simply have a great time!

8. **Related Sales Teams.** Talking to people who are successful in a SIMILAR business but don't offer the same services can be productive in a couple of ways. They might pay you to do things for their clients while taking the credit, but sharing the profits. They also might refer clients to you if you offer a 10-20% referral fee.

9. **Join "Power" Organizations.** Participate in the same business organizations as the influencers (Rotary, industry-related groups, American Marketing Association, etc.). Often, it's as much a matter of who you know as what you know.

Ways to Approach Them

1. **Personal Touch.** After reading as much as you can about them, point out ways they could be improving their marketing. Don't be afraid to "reveal" too much. Begin teaching and offering suggestions. It will be refreshing and intriguing for many of the people you contact. If they steal your ideas and don't use you, then that's their loss. You will have come from a place of integrity and will learn something each time you do this.

2. **Financial Expectations.** Make your financial expectations high, but offer a trial period at a discount to prove yourself.

3. **What Should I Say?** During your initial e-mail or phone call, keep it simple and to the point. It doesn't matter that you offer a lot of services. Get to the bottom line on the initial contact. "Here is what I can do for you." Give a handful of examples if you have them, and

offer to send additional ones. Be enthusiastic and confident. It comes across even in an email.

4. **What if They Say They Already Have a Team of In-House Experts?** Let them know you are available to help the team out when they are overwhelmed or on vacation, and that you feel you have specific ideas that the team might find interesting. Bringing new blood into an organization can be a very positive thing, especially if you offer the discounted trial period so they could see what you can contribute.

5. **Your LinkedIn Presence.** Make sure your LinkedIn presence is up-to-date and impressive, listing many successful clients, your education, and your experience. Be sure to include the link in your contact information.

6. **Other Social Media Links.** Whether or not you're pitching them regarding their social media, make sure you have active and impressive business pages on at least Twitter, Facebook, and Google+, and include a link to them in your contact information.

7. **Do You Skype?** If you feel comfortable Skyping, let the prospective client know that. It's just like having an in-person interview ... even if your client wants to introduce you to personnel in other locations around the world.

8. **Your Website.** It is absolutely essential that you have a professional website that tells who you are and what you do, plus educates the visitor in the blog posts.

9. **Publish An E-Book.** If you are a published author regarding the skills you are making available, it adds to your credibility.

10. **Focus On Specific Projects.** Find out what type of projects they are working on. Watch for an opening to discover some way you can help them.

11. **The Best Approach.** When you meet people at events or online, don't pitch your services. Instead, be the expert on your subject. Offer concrete suggestions, presenting perhaps a bigger and better picture of ways they could be branding themselves or improving their ecommerce or traffic. Give them a card and offer to chat anytime they have questions.

12. **Solve Their Problems.** Don't try to sell them a service. Offer to help solve their problems.

13. **Offer to Consult.** You can also provide a consultation service. If they feel they have a good enough team in place, show them one aspect where you can teach and guide their team to even greater success. Once you've demonstrated good results, they'll use your expertise more and more.

14. **What If They Say No?** Not everyone is going to say yes! But you don't need very many big clients to ultimately get you a six-figure annual income. Have patience and perseverance and you will prevail!

When you're moving up the food chain to close bigger and more lucrative clients, remember that they are just people like you and me who have problems to solve and are looking for a great solution. If you can provide that solution, you will have a lucrative client for many years to come.

Best of luck in your move up the food chain!

About the Author

A former executive for IBM, AT&T, and NEC, Joe (JT) Ippolito is the Founder and CEO of Media Marketing Management. As an award-winning entrepreneur, business owner, speaker, author, and consultant, he specializes in cross-channel marketing strategies that help companies increase their revenue with his proprietary tactics.

Joe has worked on complex technology solutions with C-level executives in boardroom settings. Having received numerous awards, clients have included: Disney, Mattel, Sony, Warner Bros., and Fox.

A self-styled "media disrupter," Joe's ideas challenge the status quo of new media marketing. For 34 years, he's dedicated his career to his unique brand of high-leverage marketing, bringing great success to former employers and dozens of name brand clients.

As his goals have evolved, Ippolito is now focused on nurturing the entrepreneur in anyone—especially men and women who are convinced that it's too late in their careers to change directions. He made the same leap himself, bringing his broad corporate experience to eager new business owners for a fraction of his cost.

"When I was in school, I did not do very well. I graduated in the part of my class that made the top 90% possible.

"I have reinvented myself many times over the years. I am a recovering executive for three publicly-traded technology companies.

"When I first stepped away from my role at IBM, I reveled in the freedom. I felt a little fear, to be sure. But mostly, I was excited about doing what I loved, and leaving behind the corporate bureaucracy and the non-stop parade of meetings.

"I want everyone to experience that kind of freedom."

We believe in giving back when there is no immediate opportunity for return, "paying it forward" with startup companies, with entrepreneurs that are trying to metamorphose ideas into businesses, and with young professionals who are trying to find their path in life.

See his books on Amazon.com:

Encore Entrepreneurs: The Baby Boomer's Guide to Reinventing Your Life (The Reinvention of Your Business Pedigree)

Big Marketing Ideas for Small Marketing Budgets: Online Strategies for Getting More Local Business FAST

Visit his websites:

http://www.mediamarketingmgmt.com
http://www.jtippolito.com

Putting it all together: A Case Study—Magna Wave Certification Process
by Pat Ziemer

In 2007, I started working with a high-powered pulsed electro-magnetic therapy device (PEMF) providing therapy to racehorses and performance horses around the country. I was already working in the horse industry selling therapy devices, but with this new device, which we called Magna Wave, I was actually providing the therapy treatments. My providing the treatments was an obstacle because I was known around the country as an equipment salesman and not a therapist. Consequently some people felt that I did not have the qualifications to be a therapist. I did have a secondary college degree in the areas of physiology, anatomy, and pathology so I spoke of that as a basis for my understanding and providing the therapy. While that story helped the cause, the real catalyst in the business growth was that the therapy really worked. In the beginning, I was the "crazy guy" pulling around this new therapy machine. Then I became "Dr. Voodoo" with this weird machine that did seem to work. Then I became the guy that veterinarians considered competition and it must be potentially harmful or at best illegal. The therapy became so popular that the veterinary community, for the most part, embraced it.

In the beginning, my wife and I traveled the country in an RV providing treatments. We were starting to do well and as you might suspect, people began inquiring about purchasing machines to provide the therapy. I did not know where this would go, but I began selling the machines and training the new practitioners. It seemed that wherever we would travel, we would find someone wanting to purchase the equipment and begin working their own customers. Training was not an issue, because I was there treating the horses, which provided the perfect way to train the new machine owners. Over the next three years, we grew to nearly 100 practitioners around the country and I had to quit treating so as to not compete with the new practitioners.

By this time, our business revenue had grown to the mid- to upper-six figures and it seemed to plateau there for three years. I knew that I needed to beef up the training and I wanted to offer training and certification as part of the program. I worked with several different platforms, but I just could not get the system going. The work and time involved seemed insurmountable. I was actively working the Internet and social networks in order to grow the business because we learned that our primary customers, horsemen and horsewomen, were active on sites like Facebook. It was late in 2011 when I discovered Mike Keonigs and Instant Customer. I bought into the system in order to use it to better market our products, our practitioners, and also use it for other businesses. The marketing for other businesses was a mistake because it took my focus away from Magna Wave. Along the way, I became certified in Mike's AEMM program because I was going to again use the product for others. While at one of Mike's events, I was sitting in a gathering of people that ultimately became a mastermind group of those who wrote this book you are reading. I was discussing my need for a certification program when one member of the group looked at me and said, "You can build the program within Instant Customer and AEMM, just duplicate the way they do it." I was dumbfounded, Could it really be that easy?

Within a week of my returning home from the event, the basis of my own certification program was in place. The next thing I had to do was work out the logistics of promotion videos, recording the webinars, editing, hosting, SEO, and a myriad of other details. Ultimately, I sought out the help of those who wrote this book for guidance on each step of the way in producing the Magna Wave certification program. This group suggested what programs to use and in most cases helped me avoid learning curves in order to get quick implementation. The bones were in place in two weeks, the program was launched within four weeks, and the live webinar classes were completed, recorded, and edited within ten weeks. The program has been in evergreen mode for the past year and a half. I am now in the process of redoing the program and adding modules for humans and small animals. So the question is, how did the program affect the business?

The impact was immediate and dramatic. Over the first 30 to 60 days, sales were up 40% and the driving force was the certification process. Some racing jurisdictions actually require the certification for access to the grounds with our type of device. We became the experts in the field and our credibility and respect increased proportionately. This momentum drove the business to seven figures and we are well on our way to doubling our sales, with a goal of reaching the mid-seven figures within the next five years.

I continue to meet with my mastermind group weekly and I ask questions pertaining to what I am currently working to accomplish. The answers I receive continue to give me direction and cut implementation time in half or more. You, too, can benefit from this brain trust of experts in the ever-changing world of Internet and offline marketing. You cannot ask and spend the time or you can ask and save time and make more money. My accountant used to tell me it is not how fast you find the hole, it's how fast you fill it. Shovels are ready, how can we help?

About the Author

Pat Ziemer is the owner of Magna Wave. The company's therapy devices are used extensively on racehorses, performance horses, and professional athletes. Five recent Kentucky Derby winners and numerous world champions in many horse disciplines utilize the therapy regularly. In 2007, Pat acquired the rights to the PEMF device, repackaged it, branded it as Magna Wave and hit the road marketing the Magna Wave brand. Since 2007, Pat has placed over 400 Magna Wave devices into the market for private and professional use, primarily in the equine marketplace. The company is now moving into the areas of human and small animal therapy.

www.MagnaWavePEMF.com
PatZiemer@MagnaWavePEMF.com

Final Thoughts

IT'S YOUR MOVE...

Now that you have had a chance to glance/read/study this book, it's time to make a decision AND... take action.

LONE WOLF vs FINDING A COACH

There are a few of us that have been able to purchase, study, and succeed, all in the confines of our own home or business. There are LOTS of us that realized we should have hired a coach.

If you are looking to start or build your business and make it a HUGE success, and are looking for direction—we can help.

Simply go to http://www.hotseatpanel.com and select from a variety of options we've designed especially for you.

Wishing you the very best,

Karol Clark	Everett O'Keefe
Rob Cuesta	Cydney O'Sullivan
Jerry Dreessen	Dave Pittman
Niki Faldemolaei	Melodie Rush
JT Ippolito	Carl Stearns
Steve Laurvick	Steve Walther
Sandi Masori	Pat Ziemer

www.ingramcontent.com/pod-product-compliance
Lightning Source LLC
Chambersburg PA
CBHW071412170526
45165CB00001B/248